MANAGING
FINANCE
AND
INFORMATION

MANAGING
FINANCE
AND
INFORMATION

Ron Simpson

B.Ed., M.Sc, MBCS

PITMAN
PUBLISHING

London · Hong Kong · Johannesburg · Melbourne · Singapore · Washington DC

PITMAN PUBLISHING
128 Long Acre, London WC2E 9AN
Tel: +44 (0)171 447 2000
Fax: +44 (0)171 240 5771

A Division of Pearson Professional Limited

First published in Great Britain in 1997

© Pearson Professional Limited 1997

The right of Ron Simpson to be identified as Author
of this Work has been asserted by him in accordance
with the Copyright, Designs and Patents Act 1988.

ISBN 0 273 62637 X

British Library Cataloguing in Publication Data
A CIP catalogue record for this book can be obtained from the British Library

10 9 8 7 6 5 4 3 2 1

Typeset by M Rules, London
Printed and bound in Great Britain by Clays Ltd, St Ives plc

The Publishers' policy is to use paper manufactured from sustainable forests.

Contents

Contents

Preface

'We live in the information age.' How often are we told this these days? It is as if the whole planet were 'wired up' and 'hanging out', waiting for the next satellite bulletin or news-bite, the next e-mail or Internet page, the next digital voice or video. In fact, most of us feel we are in danger of missing out. We try to keep up – only to find the virtual goal-posts moving (in 3D simulation) as we line up to take our shot.

This anxiety of the individual is replicated in the world of business. Few companies are without some worry that they may be left behind, or upstaged, by a competitor. Indeed, many are so fearful (or, perhaps, so smitten by the apparent wonders of technology) they will seemingly pay any price to grasp the latest product, sometimes before it is tried and tested, and even on occasion before anyone can think of a valid use for it.

Of course, you and I know – as does any successful business executive – that the real lifeblood of any business is not information but cash. Nonetheless, one of the aims of this book is to make the argument that cash *without* information might as well be under the mattress, whereas information without cash, at least, possesses potential.

The text covers all the course requirements of BTEC Higher National Diploma and Certificate courses in Business – Core Module Four: 'Managing Finance and Information'.

It is also aimed at all students of business who need to integrate a knowledge of business computing with that of financial management. In addition, it will be of interest to those undertaking professional studies in financial or information systems management.

The main objective throughout has been to produce a substantive but concise book which, above all, is readable. Additional study material, assignments and case studies are included to cover the BTEC content and intended learning outcomes, but these do not invade the text, which is intended to be read for interest as well as to be worked from.

Ron Simpson
January 1997

Part One

MANAGING FINANCE

1 Cost and cash flow

Learning objectives

◆ To differentiate types of business cost and define relevant cost.

◆ To identify relationships between:
  - fixed cost
  - variable cost
  - sales volume
  - sales value
  - selling price
  - profit
  - loss
  - breakeven.

◆ To draw a breakeven chart from relevant data and calculate breakeven in terms of volume sales.

◆ To identify the criteria involved in sales forecasting.

◆ To outline the main responsibilities, skills and knowledge involved in financial management.

◆ To understand the cyclical nature of business operations and activity.

◆ To understand the importance of working capital, cash flow and cash management.

◆ To create a cash flow forecast from relevant figures.

◆ To outline how a company manages its debtors.

◆ To identify ways in which businesses can achieve optimum stock levels.

The primary activity of a business is to produce goods or services for its customers by consuming resources (at a cost). Profit is made for as long as the cost of this consumption remains lower than the revenue returns from production. The management, measurement and analysis of costs and revenue, together with the associated cash flows, is therefore fundamental to business and financial management. It is also an important element in any evaluation of financial performance.

In this opening chapter, we start with the nature of cost. We will then go on to examine its relationship with revenue and with other financial components. It is the mix of all of these factors which determines a business's profitability or loss.

Types of cost

Although several of the categories overlap, there are a number of different ways in which financial managers and analysts differentiate cost.

Resource costs

Materials

These are costs incurred through the consumption (in production) of:

◆ *raw materials* (e.g. crude oil in petroleum production);
◆ *semi-processed or part-finished goods* (e.g. spun and woven textiles involved in printing);
◆ *fully-finished goods (components)* (e.g. automotive parts – such as safety airbags – in motor vehicle assembly).

Materials costs may also be incurred by non-manufacturing (service) companies. For example, laundries consume washing powder, garages consume oil.

Labour

Labour is the most significant cost for the majority of businesses. It includes:

◆ wages;
◆ National Insurance, sickness and holiday pay;
◆ pension contributions;
◆ health and safety;
◆ training;
◆ redundancy and severance payments.

Expenses

These are best defined as costs not attributable to either labour or materials. It is an extremely wide category, covering all those costs not directly contributing, but essential, to the production process. Some examples are:

◆ power;

◆ rent and rates;

◆ equipment depreciation;

◆ sales and marketing expenses;

◆ travel and subsistence;

◆ vehicle expenses;

◆ insurance premiums.

Direct and indirect costs

Direct costs

These are *prime* costs in that they are integral to the actual production of goods or services which are being supplied. This means that the effect, on direct costs, of any rise or fall in the level of production, will be proportional, predictable and relatively easy to quantify or allocate. For example, a car assembly plant will consume spark plugs and windscreen glass in direct proportion to the number of vehicles produced, the only variable being a possible renegotiation of price if volumes rise markedly. In a service industry such as hairdressing, the cost of shampoo solutions is going to vary (more or less) in proportion to the number of heads coming through the door.

Indirect costs

These are often referred to as *overheads* or expenses. They are incurred in association with, but not in direct relation to, the level of production. For example, the consumption of power to heat and light an office can be related to the number of visiting clients only to the extent that (at the extremes) it may be necessary to open up more space or it is possible to close early. Power is a cost which must be borne at (or around) the same amount, irrespective of production. In a manufacturing company, the relationship may be stronger. In a car assembly plant, power consumption will correlate positively to the number of cars made. However, because of the difficulty of allocating specific costs to the different functions or departments of a business, indirect costs are normally measured in some proportion to direct costs. In this example, electricity costs might be calculated at a certain ratio to man- or machine-hours (Fig. 1.1). Other indirect costs may also be allocated in similar ways, allowing them to be included in the overall cost of the product.

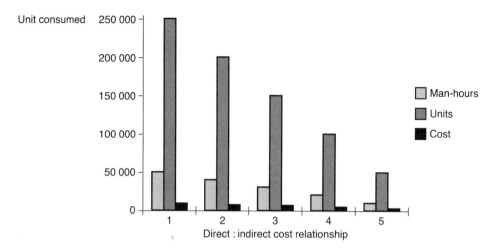

Fig 1.1   Ratio of direct to indirect costs: man-hours : power consumption and costs

Fixed and variable costs

Fixed costs

These are costs which, over the short term at least, are invariable (Fig. 1.2). Rent, rates and loan interest must be paid whatever the level of business activity. In the long term, of course, even these are likely to change as loans are repaid, interest rates change or rents are renegotiated.

Variable costs

These correlate strongly and positively with production levels (Fig. 1.2). In the short term, it is possible to consider even these as fixed costs, since, in most cases, business activity is likely to remain relatively stable over short periods of time. In most respects, however, they are properly seen as variable – either continuously variable, or stepped in some way. For example, each new car needs five wheels. Consequently, an increase in production from 100 to 200 vehicles per month will cause a proportional increase in wheel consumption. The relationship is direct and continuous. On the other hand, the rise in production may necessitate an increase in direct labour costs proportional to only 0.5 of an employee. Unless a 'half-person' (top or bottom?) is hanging (standing?) around waiting to be hired, it is unlikely that labour costs will remain in direct proportion, although, over time, the curve will smooth out.

Avoidable and unavoidable costs

Avoidable costs

This category theoretically includes *all* variable costs. A fleet of company cars, for example, will incur fuel charges to the extent they are used, but a decision could be made to eliminate or reduce the cost if desired.

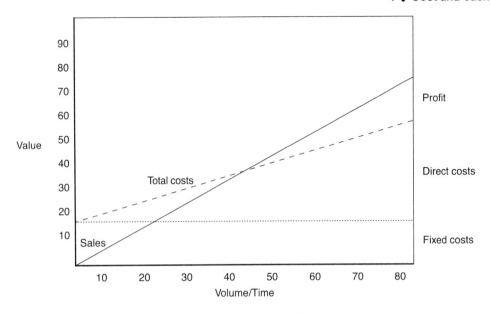

Fig 1.2   Fixed and variable costs, sales and profits

Some fixed costs are also avoidable. Using the same example, service charges and road fund licenses would still need to be paid whether or not the cars are driven. However, the cost is still avoidable if the vehicles are sold.

Unavoidable costs

These are fixed costs which have to be paid whatever short-term decisions are made, the best example being building maintenance charges.

Relevant cost

This is not another category of cost so much as an imperative to include only those costs which are *relevant* to the particular task or decision which is at hand. For example, a decision to fax someone rather than post them a letter would not be taken on the basis of a single instance, and from a single calculation of the telephone call charge as opposed to postage. It is the relevant costs which matter, and these are those costs which are actually affected by the decision. Once the initial cost, depreciation and maintenance of the fax machine are included, it may be that the postman seems the better choice – especially for large items, sporadic usage or non-urgent documents. On the other hand, the relevant costs of posting a letter do not just include the price of the stamp. Nor can the fixed costs associated with owning a fax machine be avoided merely by not using it.

To take another example, what are the relevant costs surrounding a decision whether to buy or rent a personal computer?

Buy	*Rent*
Purchase price	Rent
VAT	Support
Delivery	
Installation	
Interest	
Maintenance	
Support	
Depreciation	
Rising inefficiency due to obsolescence	

Why do most people buy? Have they compared the relevant costs?

The measurement and analysis of relevant costs and any associated revenues is appropriate to any decision which has to take account of the dynamic relationships which exist between fixed and variable costs, production level, selling price, sales volume and value, profit and loss. Such decisions are, of course, fundamental to business and financial management.

A simple example will illustrate the basic relationships involved. Suppose that, via a combination of customer survey and past experience, garden gnome manufacturer, Zurich Gnomes, forecasts the following sales at different selling prices:

Selling price *£*	*Forecast sales per month* *(Units)*
40	10 000
50	9 000
60	8 000
70	6 500
80	5 500
90	4 000

Fixed costs	= £60 000 per month
Variable costs	= £30 per unit

What is the most favourable selling price?

Selling price *£*	*Sales* *£*	*Fixed costs* *£*	*Variable costs* *£*	*Revenue from sales* *£*
40	400 000	60 000	300 000	40 000
50	450 000	60 000	270 000	120 000
60	480 000	60 000	240 000	180 000
70	455 000	60 000	195 000	200 000
80	440 000	60 000	165 000	215 000
90	360 000	60 000	120 000	180 000

This kind of exercise is, unfortunately, a bit awkward in all but the simplest of cases. An alternative is to work out the ratio of direct to indirect costs for each product. This will then hold for any similar calculation to give a rapid indication of likely returns.

In the garden gnome example, we would have:

		£
Direct cost per unit (gnome)	=	30
Direct cost (10 000 units)	=	300 000
Indirect costs	=	60 000
Total costs	=	360 000
Therefore:		$\dfrac{60\ 000}{300\ 000} \times 100 = 20\%$

Indirect costs are equal to 20 per cent of direct costs for this particular product.

Breakeven analysis

Breakeven analysis defines the point at which sales revenues are equal to total costs (fixed and variable). Its significance as an indicator of financial performance and health lies in its ready portrayal of:

◆ the level of financial risk;
◆ breakeven point (time) – i.e. the point in time that sales will cover costs;
◆ breakeven point (volume) – i.e. the volume of sales required to cover costs;
◆ its underlying prediction of cash flow (more of this later);
◆ its usefulness in many business management and planning tasks.

It is normal practice to chart breakeven. The chart can represent an entire business or be drawn for a particular project to see if it is viable. The example shown in Fig. 1.3 is typical for a small business. It shows a breakeven point for a start-up business approximately five months into the first year of operation. In general, the nearer the point is to the vertical axis, the less the risk and the greater the profitability. In this case, the business is initially vulnerable, as are most new businesses or projects.

In some cases, what is required is a quick comparison of different business projects by calculating breakeven in terms of volume sales.

For example, a product has direct costs of £45 and is sold for £50. We know that this will not produce a profit of £5 because we have not yet accounted for indirect costs. However, provided each individual sale at least covers the direct costs it incurs, it can be seen to have made some *contribution* to fixed costs and profits – it has achieved a gross profit equal to sales revenue minus direct cost.

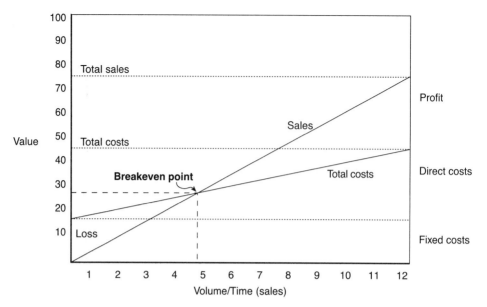

Fig 1.3   Breakeven chart

The breakeven point (volume) can therefore be calculated as:

$$\frac{\textbf{Fixed costs}}{\textbf{Contribution of each sale}}$$

It should be clear from all this that breakeven analysis portrays the position a business may reach at a particular time. It is not a picture of actual performance but of possible (probable) scenarios, which may be realised under certain conditions, and if particular business decisions are made.

 ## Sales forecasting

Although breakeven analysis will tell a business what volume of sales is required to stay in business, it is really no more than the portrayal of a mathematical relationship. It is not even a forecast of what will (or may) happen. To do this with any degree of accuracy requires experience and market knowledge – even a little intuition.

Forecasts and confidence

The degree of confidence we have in the predictive powers of any forecast is likely to depend on:

◆ *the context* – some things are inherently easier to predict than others (e.g. it is relatively safe to predict that in any Olympic games, the USA will have more medal winners than the UK);

◆ *the forecaster* – some are (or seem to be) more expert than others (e.g. we will probably have more confidence in a weather forecast from the Meteorological Office than one based on granny's arthritic toe);

◆ *the lead time* – the longer this is, the less confidence we have (e.g. Met Office forecasts are very accurate up to 24 hours, less so over 48 or 72 hours, and no better than granny's toe for a period of more than seven days).

Forecasts based on previous results

Businesses produce sales forecasts, not sales *plans*. In so doing, they recognise that the level of sales eventually reached is determined by factors largely beyond their control. They can, of course, limit sales by reducing production or increasing price – as they can probably increase sales by reducing price. But these are only blunt instruments. In reality, sales volumes will be determined more by economic trends, income levels, competitor activity, public taste and perceptions of quality. Here again, the business can influence but not dictate results. For example, a significant increase in product quality reinforced by extra sales and marketing effort may lead to increased sales – albeit at additional cost.

The forecasting of sales, consequently, is as much art as science, in that it relies to such an extent on particular experience.

The known parameters will usually be:

◆ *previous sales results;*
◆ *current product sales trends* (i.e. are they stable, rising or falling?);
◆ *current market trends* (i.e. is it flat, growing or depressed?);
◆ *current economic trends* (i.e. growth, recession, income levels, etc.);
◆ *any seasonal factors* (e.g. summer sales of ice cream or soft drinks).

Once these parameters are quantified in some way and then tabulated, it is possible to extrapolate to a prediction, and view the effects on this prediction of any variability in any of the parameters. (This is particularly easy to do if a computerised spreadsheet is employed – more on this later.)

As an example, let us assume a company has steady, long-term growth in sales volume of around 3 per cent per annum. This is readily extrapolated to a forecast for next year (*see* Table 1.1).

Forecasts based on market research

What if a business is a start-up, and cannot extrapolate in this way. It must then (from its initial market research) find evidence which points towards a particular level of sales as being attainable. This might be done via an analysis of competitors and from sample surveys of potential customers.

Table 1.1   Sales forecast (volume)

	CY – 5	CY – 4	CY – 3	CY – 2	CY – 1	Current year (CY)	Forecast (CY + 1)
April	419	432	447	461	477	491	506
May	480	494	512	528	546	563	580
June	532	548	567	585	605	624	643
July	432	445	461	475	491	507	522
August	581	598	619	639	661	681	702
September	543	559	579	597	618	637	656
October	421	434	449	463	479	494	509
November	852	878	908	937	969	999	1029
December	984	1014	1049	1083	1119	1154	1189
January	345	355	368	380	392	405	417
February	298	307	318	328	339	350	360
March	364	375	388	400	414	427	440

Using this as a basis it is then possible to:

◆ estimate the average monthly sales volume;

◆ adjust this to take account of any seasonal factors;

◆ adjust this to make allowance for start-up – i.e. the business will take some time to 'get up to speed';

◆ make a forecast based on these parameters (*see* Table 1.2).

Table 1.2   Start-up sales forecast

Start-up	Forecast	Start-up (%)	Adjusted	Seasonal (%)	Adjusted forecast
April	500	–90	50		50
May	500	–80	100		100
June	500	–60	200		200
July	500	–40	300		300
August	500	–20	400		400
September	500	–10	450		450
October	500		500	+30	650
November	500		500	+60	800
December	500		500	+90	950
January	500		500	+20	600
February	500		500		500
March	500		500		500

Financial management

So far, we have concentrated on the processes of allocating cost and relating this to revenue. All but the smallest businesses employ professional accountants and associated clerical staff to manage and carry through these processes. At the higher levels of financial management, minds are concentrated on the primary objective of maximising profit in relation to resources consumed. As we have seen, this consumption involves different types of cost and presents differing implications for a business's short-term performance and for its long-term progress and survival. This cost–return relationship is also often the result of some balancing, within an organisation, of conflicting factors or aspirations. What might maximise profit in the short term may not achieve the same result in the long run. Nor will an objective to reduce interest costs by repaying loans early be of much benefit to a company if the undue strain this puts on cash reserves causes the business to become insolvent.

Financial managers serve to provide this balance. Sometimes the competing (and, possibly, conflicting) objectives are presented to them by other managers. Sometimes they may even override the primary aim of profit maximisation, in reflecting personal or corporate ambition and power, or in representing equally non-optimising caution and aversion to risk.

The ideal knowledge and skills base of the individuals given this responsibility is (as in most areas of management) both wide and deep. It should certainly include a knowledge of the following topics.

◆ *Management accounting.* This includes skills and techniques which allow comparative analysis of costs, cash inflow and outflow, and profitability. This, in turn, involves estimates of fixed and variable costs, and the continual monitoring of performance to provide early warning of any failure to stay with agreed objectives, or within agreed limits. There is also an important element of negotiation and liaison with the different departments and functions of an organisation to ensure realistic budgets are set and adhered to, and that set objectives are realistic and attainable.

◆ *Financial accounting.* This involves the collection, compilation and summarisation of financial figures, and includes:

– current cash balances and assets;

– costs and acquisitions;

– sales;

– profit or loss;

– share holdings, tax, debt and other liabilities.

This is a vital service for all businesses, and (as we will see later) is a legal requirement for companies whose shares are traded on the stock market.

◆ *Company law and taxation.*

◆ *Economics and related political matters.*

Business operation

Financial managers and accountants do not, of course, ponder over these concerns merely in abstraction and in theory. Unless a business is at start-up, they will be embroiled within a continuous cycle of activity, which pushes the company along its chosen path and (hopefully) towards the achievement of its planned objectives.

This day-to-day business functioning is, to some extent, cyclical (*see* Figs 1.4 and 1.5). It is financed by capital which, because it must remain fluid and related to volumes of work (i.e. material supplies, labour, production and sales), is referred to as *working capital*.

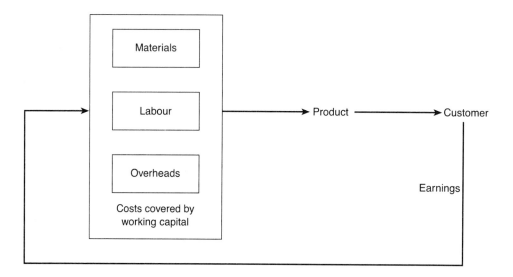

Fig 1.4   Business operating cycle

The management of working capital is a crucial part of business and financial management, and we will return to it in more detail a little later on. Let us, first, consider some related constituent elements of business operation and activity.

Capital investment cycle

Investment in fixed assets is usually uneven. In some industries, such as aerospace, telecommunications or oil exploration, expenditures on fixed assets can be huge – look, for example, at BT's expenditure over a five-year period (1992–6):

Expenditure on tangible fixed assets
Year Ended 31 March

	1992 £m	1993 £m	1994 £m	1995 £m	1996 £m
Plant and equipment					
Transmission	1 173	835	896	1 060	1 114
Telephone exchanges	722	545	493	605	566
Other network equip.	281	296	335	378	491
Computers and office	170	152	219	343	333
Motor vehicles etc.	131	272	153	214	195
Land and buildings	54	66	51	75	87
Increase (decrease) in stores	(85)	(11)	24	(4)	(15)
Total expenditure	2 446	2 155	2 171	2 671	2 771
Decrease (increase) in creditors	119	(7)	(10)	(33)	(224)
Cash outflow	2 565	2 148	2 161	2 638	2 547

Source: British Telecommunications plc, *Financial Review* (1996).

This size of capital investment is very large and may have an impact on cash reserves and working capital for several years afterwards. In other industries, the lead times are not so long, but it can still be a problem for companies if they are required to make abnormal, irregular expenditures out of normal, regular income. One answer is to raise share capital (*see* Chapter 2), another is to lease the required asset, or finance it from a loan repayable over the asset's useful lifespan.

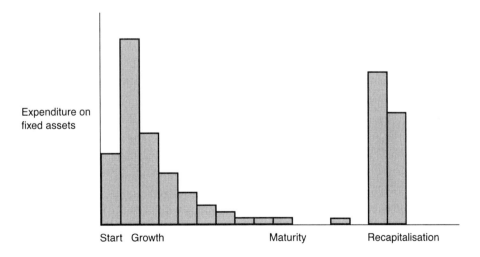

Fig 1.5   Capital investment cycle

Product lifecycle

New products usually run at a loss – at least through their design, development and marketing stages (*see* Fig. 1.6). All these attract costs, but there will, of course, be no returns until sales are made. If a business is continually developing new products in this way, it must allow for this cycle of expenditure and reduced sales revenues in its calculations for capital requirement.

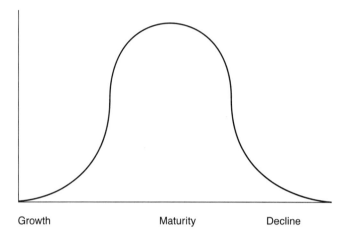

Growth   Maturity   Decline

Fig 1.6   Product lifecycle

Trading level

The volume of trade should clearly be at the highest possible level consistent with the business remaining able to finance its costs, while waiting for income. Businesses quite frequently fail because of *overtrading*, i.e. they are too successful in terms of sales growth (but not in converting sales into revenue) and run out of the finance to maintain production at a level which would satisfy demand.

Trading cycle

If the volume of trade is affected by seasonal (or other) factors which make sales volumes and/or revenues uneven, this also needs to be accommodated in capital requirements.

A couple of examples will serve to illustrate some of the difficulties businesses can find themselves in if any of these factors are ignored.

Shady-Sun is a sun-bed assembly business, set up in rented premises and financed from a bank loan of £5000 repayable in full after 12 months. As Table 1.3 shows, the business is successful in terms of growing sales. But is its provision of working capital adequate to maintain supplies and to repay its bank loan on time?

Table 1.3   Shady-Sun trading balances

	Jan £	Feb £	Mar £	Apr £	May £	Jun £	Jul £	Aug £	Sep £	Oct £	Nov £	Dec £	Total £
Orders			250	750	750	750	1000	1000	2000	2000	2500	2500	13 500
Sales income				250	500	750	750	1000	1000	1750	2000	2250	10 250
Materials	3000			750			750			1000			5 500
Overheads	300	300	300	300	300	300	300	300	300	300	300	300	3 600
Profit/loss	–3300	–300	–300	–800	200	450	–300	700	700	450	1700	1950	1 150
Balance	1700	1400	1100	300	500	950	650	1350	2050	2500	3300	4250	4 250

(Opening balance = £5000)

Our second example, *Crisis Computers*, is a direct supplier of desk-top computer systems and software. Because of severe competition, the business has traded with only small profit margins for the last three years. However, with strict economies and efficiency gains, it has so far managed to remain solvent and even to pay off its start-up bank loan on time. Unfortunately, this is, to some extent, offset by maximum use of overdraft arrangements.

Crisis has recently been flooded with orders for computers containing much more memory than was formerly required. The owners know this is because of new operating systems and other software applications that demand more memory to run satisfactorily. They also know that they have been slow to react to this change.

Unfortunately, although memory prices have been low in the recent past, they are now rising sharply as demand exceeds supply. Having failed to build up any stock when prices were low and supply plentiful, the company is now faced with high components costs to meet the new demand. Furthermore, because of their competitors' practice of giving credit to customers, Crisis has been forced to do likewise and has also picked up some bad debts. Order books are full – albeit for a different product specification than supplied in the past. However, component suppliers require payment before allowing further delivery; customers want products but will only pay at delivery plus the customary credit period. The bank is not prepared to risk a further loan to the company, given the history of low margins and extensive competition. It finally loses confidence altogether, and calls in its overdraft. The company is insolvent because it has run out of working capital.

Cash flow and budgets

Cash flow forecasts

Insolvency is the result not of a lack of assets but of a lack of *liquid* assets, i.e. cash, or assets that can be readily exchanged for cash. The importance, to any business, of its awareness of cash flow is consequently difficult to overstate.

Cash flow statements are an important indicator of company viability. They are, in fact, a legal requisite for companies whose shares are offered to the public. Anyone wishing to raise finance for a business idea will be asked, not only to forecast sales and profits, but also to predict cash flows in and out of the business over the succeeding six or 12 months. Forecasts are normally updated each month to take account of what actually happens (*see* Table 1.4).

Table 1.4   Cash flow forecast

	April		May		June	
	Forecast	Actual	Forecast	Actual	Forecast	Actual
	£	£	£	£	£	£
Sales	5 000		5 000		5 000	
Debts collected	2 500		2 500		2 500	
Total receipts	*7 500*		*7 500*		*7 500*	
Materials	2 700		2 700		2 700	
Wages	1 500		1 500		1 500	
Capital items	3 750					
Overheads	1 000		600		600	
Drawings	2 000		2 000		2 000	
Total payments	*10 950*		*6 800*		*6 800*	
Net inflow/outflow	–3 450		700		700	
Opening balance	8 250		4 800		8 500	
Closing balance	*4 800*		*5 500*		*9 200*	

Cash budgeting

If a business is to maximise its cash balances it needs to:

◆ spread the cost of fixed assets over their useful lifespan, either through leasing arrangements, hire-purchase or long-term loans;

◆ minimise stocks;

◆ invoice for payment immediately on delivery;

◆ maximise credit from suppliers;

◆ minimise credit to customers;

◆ minimise bad debt.

It should not, however, build up such positive cash balances that cash is lying around unused – especially if this is in a non-interest-bearing, current account.

Cash budgeting should ensure:

◆ all necessary materials or components are purchased as required;

◆ overheads are paid as and when due;

◆ labour costs are covered on due dates;

◆ tax and other liabilities such as loans can be paid on time;

◆ debtors (particularly bad debts) do not become an undue burden.

Average working capital requirement

In addition to the projection of working capital requirements over time, it may also be helpful to calculate an *average* requirement (*see* Table 1.5). The resulting figure may then be regarded as a permanent investment in the business – to be financed also in a permanent way, for example from retained earnings, share capital or long-term loan. (We will look at these in the next chapter.)

Table 1.5   Average working capital requirement

Average value of current assets	£
Raw materials and components in stock	30 000
Finished goods in stock	50 000
Fixed overheads	10 000
Debtors	40 000
Average value of current liabilities	130 000
Creditors	40 000
Average requirement for working capital	90 000

Debtors

Although cash payment (or substitutes, such as cheques, credit and debit cards) is normal in retail trade, most business-to-business trade involves credit, and most businesses have debtors as most have creditors.

Credit terms tend to be set on the basis of 'custom and practice'. As such, they vary from industry to industry, and with the purchasing power of large corporations. Many of these will not settle before 90 days – much to the dismay of small companies on tight finance. On the other hand, large companies, such as gas, water, telecommunications and electricity utilities, are themselves able (effectively) to give 90 days' credit to customers.

Small businesses normally trade on a 30-day basis. Many (all) would prefer cash payment, but the competition will not allow it. In general, there is little point in any one company attempting to vary the normal credit terms set by convention for their particular business. Any reduction in the credit period is only likely to result in lost orders, while the reverse might gain customers, but only at the cost of reduced working capital and an increase in bad debt.

It is fairly common practice to offer a discount for early settlement. This is effectively an addition to the cost of working capital, so it needs to be measured against the savings in administration costs from not having to chase for payment.

Bad debts

These can be kept to a minimum through credit checks and/or experience of previous business. Since chasing bad debts through the courts is a long and expensive process, companies obviously try to keep them to a minimum by:

◆ systematic 'chasing-up' policies;
◆ debt factoring (letting a specialist company take over the debt – more on this later);
◆ reserving title (ownership) of goods until full payment is received.

Stock

Stock in this respect refers to the temporary storage of materials and finished goods prior to production or sale.

Businesses can only function properly by maintaining stocks at a level sufficient to prevent delays in production or in deliveries to customers. The aim is for optimum stock levels.

If levels are too low:

◆ production may be interrupted;
◆ delivery lead times to customers may be unacceptable and lead to lost business;
◆ frequent ordering of small volumes increases administrative costs and will be less likely to attract volume discounts.

If stocks are too high:

◆ capital is tied up unnecessarily and, unless stock unit prices rise at a higher rate than any interest loss, financial penalties will be incurred;
◆ storage costs are increased and there may be a risk of deterioration or obsolescence.

How can optimum stock levels be achieved?

A prerequisite is a stock control system which allows for the recording of all stock movements and which contains data on:

◆ item code and description;
◆ quantity in stock;
◆ minimum level (reorder level);
◆ maximum level;
◆ order quantity (batch);
◆ purchase price.

The most significant figure is the reorder level. If this is set at the most economic level (we will look at a way of calculating this in Chapter 4), and administrative procedures are efficient, optimal stock levels will be attainable, if not guaranteed.

 ## Summary

◆ The fundamentals of business financial performance and survival reside in the relationship between costs and sales revenues, and the management of associated funds.

◆ Cost may be incurred through the consumption of materials, labour and various forms of expenses or overheads.

◆ The most important differentiation is between indirect and direct costs. Indirect costs are relatively fixed; direct costs vary in proportion to production levels. All variable costs are *avoidable* in theory – most fixed costs are not.

◆ Relevant costs are those which affect, and are affected by, any cost decision. Costing which initially favours one choice of expenditure may, when all relevant costs are taken into account, point to an alternative course of action.

◆ The relationships between fixed and variable costs, sales volumes, sales value, selling price, profit and loss are fundamental to business performance, and need to be quantified as accurately as possible prior to any business decision. The overall profitability and degree of risk associated with a business may be portrayed in a breakeven chart.

◆ Financial management is concerned with maximising profits in relation to resources consumed, and in achieving a balance between sometimes conflicting objectives and aspirations. The skills and knowledge base of responsible managers should include management and financial accounting, together with a relevant knowledge of company law and related economic matters.

◆ Companies need to be aware of cyclical factors which can affect this balancing of financial resources. It is perfectly possible for a business to become insolvent despite growth and full order books.

◆ Cash flow is an important indicator of financial health. In general, companies should aim to maximise liquidity without this creating unused, non-earning cash balances. Part of this process is the management of credit, debtors and stock.

Assignments

1 Identify some of the relevant costs associated with:

   ◆ owning a house;

   ◆ owning and running a car;

   ◆ marketing and publicising a business;

   ◆ going on holiday.

2 20 000 widgets at £15 each are sold each month. Widget plc estimate that price increases would vary with volume sales as follows:

Price (£)	Volume per month
12	30 000
15	20 000
17	18 000
19	12 000
20	7 000

   Fixed costs are £20 000 per month – variable cost is £10 per unit. Which is the most favourable selling price?

3 Draw a breakeven chart based on the following figures:

Fixed costs per annum	£80 000
Variable costs per product item	£40
Selling price per item	£50
Projected annual turnover	£400 000

4 If possible, ask a financial manager about his or her job, and summarise their response in terms suitable for a prospective entrant to this area of employment.

5 Cash flow forecasts can reveal as much about the state of our personal finances as of businesses. Of course, the headings will be different from a business forecast, but can you forecast your own cash flow over the next six or 12 months?

Case study

What evidence is there, in the following extracts from IBM's Financial Review 1995, to point to:

◆ falling sales, revenue and profits;

◆ cost reduction;

◆ restructuring;

◆ a readiness to expand operations;

◆ a readiness to move into new areas of service and production?

IBM Financial Highlights	Dollars in millions	
	1995	*1994*
For the year:		
Revenue	71 940	64 052
Earnings before income taxes	7 813	5 155
Income taxes	3 635	2 134
Net earnings	4 178	3 021
Per share of common stock	7.23	5.02
Cash dividends paid on common stock	572	585
Per share of common stock	1.00	1.00
Investment in plant, rental machines and other property	4 744	3 078
Average number of common shares outstanding		
(in millions)	569	585
At end of year:		
Total assets		
	80 292	81 091
Net investment in plant, rental machines and other property	16 579	16 664
Working capital	9 043	12 112
Total debt	21 629	22 118
Stockholders' equity	22 423	23 413
Number of regular, full-time employees	225 347	219 839
Number of common stockholders	668 931	713 060

Source: IBM Financial Review 1995. Reproduced with permission of IBM Corporation.

IBM Consolidated statement of operations	*Dollars in millions*		
For the year ended December 31:	*1995*	*1994*	*1993*
Revenue:			
Hardware sales	35 600	32 344	30 591
Services	12 714	9 715	9 711
Software	12 657	11 346	10 953
Maintenance	7 409	7 222	7 295
Rentals and financing	3 560	3 425	4 166
Total revenue	71 940	64 052	62 716
Cost:			
Hardware sales	21 862	21 300	20 696
Services	10 042	7 769	8 279
Software	4 428	4 680	4 310
Maintenance	3 651	3 635	3 545
Rentals and financing	1 590	1 384	1 738
Total cost	41 573	38 768	38 568
Gross profit:	30 367	25 284	24 148
Operating expenses:			
Selling, general and administrative	16 766	15 916	18 282
Research, development and engineering	6 010	4 363	5 558
Restructuring charges	—	—	8 945
Total operating expenses	22 776	20 279	32 785
Operating income (loss)	7 591	5 005	(8 637)
Other income, principally interest	947	1 377	1 113
Interest expense	725	1 227	1 273
Earnings (loss) before income taxes	7 813	5 155	(8 797)
Provision (benefit) for income taxes	3 635	2 134	(810)

Source: IBM Financial Review 1995. Reproduced with permission of IBM Corporation.

IBM Consolidated statement of cash flows	Dollars in millions		
For the year ended December 31:	1995	1994	1993
Cash flow from operating activities:			
Net earnings (loss)	4 178	3 021	(8 101)
Adjustments to reconcile net earnings (loss) to cash provided from operating activities:			
Effect of change in accounting principle	—	—	114
Effect of restructuring charges	(2 119)	(2 772)	5 230
Depreciation	3 955	4 197	4 710
Deferred income taxes	1 392	825	(1 335)
Amortisation of software	1 647	2 098	1 951
Purchased in-process research and development	1 840	—	—
(Gain) loss on disposition of fixed and other assets	(339)	(11)	151
Other changes that provided (used) cash:			
Receivables	(530)	653	1 185
Inventories	107	1 518	583
Other assets	(1 100)	187	1 865
Accounts payable	659	305	359
Other liabilities	1 018	1 772	1 615
Net cash provided from operating activities	10 708	11 793	8 327
Cash flow from investing activities:			
Payments for plant, rental machines and other property	(4 744)	(3 078)	(3 154)
Proceeds from disposition of plant, rental machines and other property	1 561	900	793
Acquisition of Lotus Development Corporation	(2 880)	—	—
Investment in software	(823)	(1 361)	(1 507)
Purchases of marketable securities and other investments	(1 315)	(3 866)	(2 721)
Proceeds from marketable securities and other investments	3 149	2 476	2 387
Proceeds from the sale of Federal Systems	—	1 503	—
Net cash used in investing activities	(5 052)	(3 426)	(4 202)
Cash flow from financing activities:			
Proceeds from new debt	6 636	5 335	11 794
Short-term borrowings less than 90 days – net	2 557	(1 948)	(5 247)
Payments to settle debt	(9 460)	(9 445)	(8 741)
Preferred stock transactions – net	(870)	(10)	1 091
Common stock transactions – net	(4 656)	318	122
Cash dividends paid	(591)	(662)	(933)
Net cash used in financing activities	(6 384)	(6 412)	(1 914)

Source: IBM Financial Review 1995. Reproduced with permission of IBM Corporation.

2 **Business and capital**

Learning objectives

◆ To distinguish between different types of business organisation and legal status.

◆ To outline the role of the major financial institutions.

◆ To compare the role of the commercial ('high street') banks with that of merchant banks.

◆ To understand why (with the exception of small businesses) commercial banks are not major providers of capital.

◆ To distinguish between different kinds of share issue.

◆ To outline the role of the Stock Exchange, stockbrokers and market makers.

◆ To understand the characteristics and relative cost of:
  – the major types of loan capital;
  – share capital;
  – current liabilities;
  – invoice factoring;
  – invoice discounting.

◆ To understand the need for a business to maintain a balanced capital structure.

◆ To calculate:
  – gearing;
  – interest cover;
  – average rate of return;
  – payback.

◆ To appreciate the strategic importance of capital investment decisions and how these may be assisted by different kinds of investment appraisal and risk assessment.

Our economy and society mirrors the natural world in many ways. A basic rule of nature is that organisms consume in order to survive, grow and reproduce. So it is with businesses. In their case, a variety of resources are consumed – and the most fundamental of these is capital.

We start this second chapter, therefore, by identifying the institutions which provide the financial framework for most businesses, and then go on to examine the nature, sources and costs of the different types of finance which are available. We will also examine the appropriate mix of finance for particular kinds of business organisation and circumstance.

Financial institutions

Commercial banks

The familiar institutions which manage our current and savings accounts conduct their business on the basic principle of lending 'short'. With the one exception of property purchase, they generally require loan repayment to be spread over no more than five years. Since many new business enterprises do not return a significant profit within this timescale, bank loans are not normally an appropriate foundation for company finance. However, they are an important source of short-term finance (in particular, of working capital), and they have an especial significance for small businesses which are just starting up.

This short-term perspective of the major banks has attracted much criticism over the years. It is generally accepted that some of the newest (and potentially most profitable) technologies do not produce any profit for five to ten years, or even longer. This leaves individuals and companies requiring investment starved of start-up funds unless these are provided out of public funds. However, in defence of the banks on this point, it may be said that basic banking practice, to a large extent, dictates this short-term philosophy.

Let us, for a moment, imagine ourselves living in the old American Wild West. It is hard to make an honest living when all around us violence and lawlessness expose the vulnerability and fragility of our efforts to make good. We, nevertheless, make our pile and want somewhere to keep it safe. Providing we have more confidence in the local bank than in the box beneath the floorboards, we deposit it there.

The bank could simply retain the cash and generate income from service charges. However, once a number of customers have made similar deposits, experience will soon suggest that not all of them are ever likely to want their money refunded at one and the same time. The bank can therefore lend quite a high percentage of the funds to other customers – at interest. Some of these borrowers will use their loans to pay for goods or services provided. Some of these may hold accounts with the same bank. The bank's reserves are consequently increased, the amount it can pay out in loans also increases, and a circulation of money is established (Fig. 2.1).

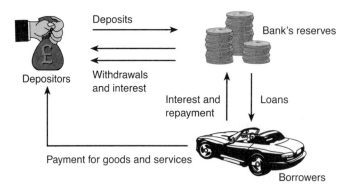

Fig 2.1   Banks and the circulation of money

This kind of financial practice is (has to be) essentially cautious and conservative. It depends in particular upon:

◆ *confidence* – deposit account holders must be sure they can withdraw in full at any time – much the same as we accept a ten-pound note in the (near) certainty it may later be exchanged, at the time of our choosing, for something of real value;

◆ *prudence* – the bank must continue to hold sensible reserves so that no depositor need ever be refused a request for withdrawal. In addition, loans must be made as risk-free as possible.

It follows, quite naturally, that banks will generally only lend on a short-term basis. This is especially true where sums are large or where no security is provided for repayment in cases of default. Given their relatively limited resources, banks which ignore this policy (and accept abnormal risk) will always be vulnerable to failure if sudden runs occur due to collapsing confidence.

Such considerations apart, commercial banks remain an important source of finance for business and are, as we have seen, especially significant for smaller companies who may have restricted access to other financial resources.

Merchant banks

In our familiar sense of the term, these are not really banks at all. They operate largely as advisors and consultants to companies wishing to raise finance or restructure themselves in some way. Some banks even specialise in turning around poorly performing companies – for example, the bankers Singer & Friedlander referred to in the *Sunday Times* article reproduced below.

Banking on a quantum leap

Platignum, the quoted stationery firm, had a poor balance sheet two years ago. Although it owned a world famous brand-name and was valued at £2 m, its largest subsidiary had just gone into receivership.

The non-executive directors turned to Singer & Friedlander, the investment bank, for advice. But instead of just doling out wise words, the bank suggested a complete management restructuring, fresh funding and then a couple of acquisitions. N trades under the name of Me and is valued at £77 m. . .

In the past couple of yea Friedlander has developed so reputation for financing risky, companies and turning them in successful enterprises that soon attract the attention of professional investors.

Source: Sunday Times, 8 December 1996. © Times Newspapers Limited, 1996.

The 'quantum leap' in the article's title refers to the dramatic turnaround in fortunes. The company's share price will, of course, reflect this, and there may also have been additional share issues made.

Share capital is referred to as *equity*. Where a company's need for finance involves a share issue, this too is often managed by a merchant bank, who will also advise on which type of issue should be made.

Public share issues

These are open to the general public. Merchant banks may even underwrite this type of issue – thereby guaranteeing its success, since they are effectively insuring against failure. In addition, the bank will also handle advertising, administration and money-processing connected with the issue. Because of these and other costs, public share issues are usually reserved for occasions when large amounts of capital need to be raised. There is often the additional desire (very evident in *privatisation* issues) to spread share ownership as widely as possible. In fact, the only constraint to distribution usually comes in the form of minimum share blocks for purchase – so avoiding trivial flirtations from individuals. In some cases, issues may be over-subscribed, with the result that prospective investors will usually be allocated fewer shares than requested.

Rights issues

In a rights issue, existing shareholders are offered further shares, often at discounted prices and in relation to their existing holding. Amounts raised will be lower than with public issues, but associated costs are much lower. Furthermore, success is more or less guaranteed, since any shareholder not wishing to take up the special offer may sell his *right* to it on the stock market.

Placings

These involve the issue of shares to specific investors (usually large institutions such as pension funds and insurance companies) who may have been encouraged to invest in a particular company through contact with a merchant bank. This is the least expensive type of share issue.

The Stock Exchange

This provides a market mechanism which brings together buyers and sellers of shares. It also deals in other forms of securities, such as debentures (more on these later). The Stock Exchange does not itself sell shares. It acts as an agency in providing the space, administrative and information systems, and professional skills necessary to conduct business. The most familiar professionals associated with the Stock Exchange are, of course, stockbrokers. However, there is a vast industry of analysts, advisors, pundits, journalists and others who make their living from the movement of shares. The most important of these are as follows.

Stockbrokers

They act in a professional capacity for clients wishing to buy or sell shares or other types of securities. Their advice should therefore be impartial of any particular investment opportunity. As is the case with lawyers or other professional practitioners, the stockbroker should always focus upon the client's needs and aspirations, and base any investment decision upon these.

Market makers

Market makers do not operate in this professional capacity and are not necessarily impartial. They buy or sell shares directly. In fact, their primary function is to buy cheap and sell dear. It is they who are approached by stockbrokers seeking to buy or sell on behalf of clients. A potential share buyer or seller is consequently faced with two sets of commission charges – first to the stockbroker who represents him, and second (indirectly) towards the market maker's 'mark-up'.

Speculators

These are market players who have no professional responsibilities and who are prepared to speculate (or gamble) on shares rising or falling during a Stock Exchange accounting period (two- or three-week sessions, ending on a Tuesday). Speculators who gamble on price rises (i.e. they buy more shares than they can afford but sell them on or before settlement day) are termed *bulls*. Those who speculate on price falls are referred to as *bears*.

Unit trusts

Unit trusts are often subsidiaries of merchant or commercial banks. They serve to spread a relatively large number of relatively small investments by aggregating these to purchase a mixed *portfolio* of shares. This mix is continually changing and may be quite widely dispersed across the economy. However, some trusts bias their dealings towards safe ('blue chip') investments; to particular sectors, such as construction and property; or to specific geographic or political units, such as the EU or South-East Asia. The primary aim is always to spread risk while achieving moderately high returns. These are distributed to the original small investors according to the number of units held.

The advantage to the investor lies in the spreading (and consequent reduction) of his risk by allowing him (indirectly) to own shares in many more companies than would otherwise be possible. Combined with the tax advantages of *personal equity plans* (PEPs) and the policy of privatisation (which has often favoured the small investor), unit trusts have done much to diversify share ownership in the UK over the past 20 years or so.

Insurance and pension funds

These are institutions which serve to convert the regular, long-term payments and savings of large numbers of individuals into either lump-sum repayments, or *annuities*. Because of the high participation rates, the funds available for reinvestment are very large. However, such is the nature of their business, these institutions will be careful to spread dealings so as to maximise benefit to customers *over the long-term*. They will usually avoid high-risk ventures and will regard themselves as successful if their total investments move (over time, in value and in income) more or less in line with the market as a whole.

Ways of raising finance

The legal framework and constitution of businesses (*see* Table 2.1) will determine, to a large extent, the ways in which they are able to satisfy their capital requirements. One major distinction is between corporate and non-corporate status.

Non-corporate businesses

These may be sole traders or partnerships. There is no legal separation between the business and its owners. Consequently, any assets or liabilities belong directly to the owners. This can be inconvenient and even dangerous where individual financial commitment in the business is at unsafe levels. The advantage is simplicity, lean administration and simpler accounting, and no dilution of control.

Table 2.1   Types of business

Effect on business	Sole trader	Partnership	Ltd and plc
Set-up	No formalities	Contract required	Registration
Control	Owner	Partners	Directors
Liability	Unlimited	Unlimited	Limited
Finance	Owner	Partners	Shares
Records	Private	Private	Public and audited
Tax etc.	Self-employed	Self-employed	Employee status
Profits	Owner	Partners	Dividends
Closure	Depends on owner	Dissolves	Continuity

Corporations

Given legal separation between the business and its owners, a company's trading activities have independent status and are not directly affected by any change in ownership. The owners (or shareholders) have assets in the business amounting to the value of their shares, and have financial commitment and liability limited to the amount they originally paid for them.

If an incorporated business is also a *public limited company (Plc)*, its shares may be offered for sale (i.e. quoted) on the stock market to the general public. Qualifying companies (based on valuation criteria and percentage public ownership) have the additional benefits of Stock Exchange listing, which eases the movement of shares, provides greater access to finance, and generally raises profile and status.

Private limited companies (Ltd) have no public share listing and generally have far fewer shareholders. They miss out on the advantages described above, but, on the other hand, are not as vulnerable to hostile takeover bids and also benefit from simpler financial reporting requirements.

Share issue is easily the most important way of financing business activity for plcs. For smaller organisations, share ownership may still be significant, although in many cases holdings will remain in just a few private hands. Alternative (or complementary) sources of business finance come in the different varieties of loan capital, and from a number of common business practices which serve to increase the amount of working capital available to a company. We will have a look at these alternatives next, and then return to equity finance to examine its particular features and characteristics.

Bank loans

We have already seen that bank loans are almost always of fixed and relatively short duration. There are a great variety of loan formats, terms and conditions, but, in general, interest rates will be set at a fixed percentage above current *base rate* and will remain fixed at that level for the duration of the loan, regardless of future base-rate changes. Additional, one-off charges may also be incurred, but this is unusual other than for secured loans. A major consideration for the would-be borrower is the emphasis the banks place on individual commitment to an enterprise. No amount of personal confidence and enthusiasm is ever going to impress a bank manager quite as much as an owner's willingness to commit his, or her, funds and assets to the business venture.

Overdrafts

Overdrafts are more flexible than ordinary loans. Interest payments may be a little higher, but there is no set pattern since banks often compete for business on the basis of special overdraft or loan arrangements – especially for new businesses. Unlike fixed-term agreements, overdrafts are repayable on demand. In practice, however, arrangements are not revoked unless agreed limits are exceeded or the bank loses confidence in the business's ability to repay. Overdrafts may be the cheapest loan alternative if cash reserves fluctuate and so reduce or eliminate the debt for periods of time.

Long-term loans

If businesses possess land and buildings these can be mortgaged to provide long-term finance, the major providers of commercial mortgages being the banks and insurance companies.

A more important method of obtaining long-term funds is through *debentures*. These are securities which (like shares) may change hands from their original holders. If the company for which debentures are held has its shares quoted on the stock market, its debentures may also be bought and sold there. Debentures also provide regular income, but (unlike shareholders, who receive dividends out of profits) debenture holders receive income as interest, and are paid in full, regardless of levels of profit or loss. Debentures may be redeemable, which means the company has agreed to buy them back at a certain date. If they are irredeemable, the holder must find a buyer if he wishes to sell. The major sources of debenture finance are investment funds and trusts, but it may also be provided by individual investors.

Smaller companies experience greater difficulty in raising long-term loans due to their lack of a proven track record and because their assets and reserves are relatively small. For this reason, the UK government provides loan guarantees for the cost of a low, fixed premium, and there are a number of start-up finance schemes available through local and regional agencies. Loan guarantees are also available from the EU, as are specific project loans from the European Regional Development Fund and the European Social Fund.

Hire-purchase and leasing arrangements

Hire-purchase allows businesses to spread the cost of an asset (usually production machinery or equipment, computer facilities or motor vehicles), and then to take ownership of the asset at the end of the agreement term – provided all payments have been made on due dates.

Leasing agreements are similar. Short-term *(operating)* leases are designed so that total payments exceed the expected depreciation of the asset while the agreement is in effect. Longer-term *(finance)* leases run for most of the useful life of the asset and are therefore designed so that total payments exceed the original cash price.

Hire-purchase and leasing finance can be obtained from banks, finance houses and leasing companies (often subsidiaries of the major banks), and from the asset suppliers themselves.

Retained earnings

This is an important source of business finance and is often (wrongly) assumed to be without cost. Some or all of a company's profits may be retained rather than being distributed to the owners. The cost comes from the increased investment that shareholders are collectively forced to make in the business. The amount is equal to that not distributed as *dividend*. This is really an *opportunity cost* since it is felt as failure to take the opportunity to reinvest or consume the income.

Liabilities

If I owe money to someone, I have a liability. If they owe me, their liability is my asset. Liabilities of any kind may be used as a form of short-term finance for as long as the business can hold out not paying them without penalty. This can apply to any kind of debt – even taxes. The most common form, however, is *trade credit* (i.e. credit given by suppliers – usually 30 days but may be longer). There is normally no cost to trade credit, except that if creditors offer discounts for early payment, then the cost is equal to the amount of discount offered. In some respects, liabilities may be viewed as long-term finance if creditors are seen as continually renewable – i.e. as one batch of creditors is paid another batch forms. This possibility notwithstanding, few businesses would view liability finance as anything more than a welcome addition to working capital.

Debt factoring

This is a way of realising an asset – in this case, debtors. If a business is experiencing difficulty recovering debt, or if it simply wants to realise it ahead of time, it can use the debt as security for obtaining a cash advance from a factoring company. There are two forms of debt factoring:

◆ *Invoice factoring* – the ownership of the whole of the debt is transferred (at a discount) to the factors in exchange for a cash advance.

◆ *Invoice discounting* – part of the debt (say, 80 per cent) is passed to the factors as a security for the advance. Ownership of the debt remains with the business as does the responsibilty for its collection. The factors are repaid as the debt is repaid.

Ordinary shares (equity finance)

All businesses try to spread risk so as to reduce their financial vulnerability in the market and to possible, unforeseen, economic change. To the extent that companies are financed by loan capital, their liability to the lender for full repayment remains with the company, or owners, regardless of income and performance. This is not true of ordinary share capital, which does not expose the business in this way because it is integrated with company fortunes. It is the ordinary shareholders who ultimately bear the risk of failure and whose income and assets are tied in with the company unless, and until, they dispose of their shares. In the case of plcs, this risk may be spread among many thousands of individual investors.

Ordinary shares have the following characteristics.

Nominal value

This is often the selling price of the shares when first issued. They may be offered:

◆ at this nominal value *(at par)*;
◆ at a higher price *(at premium)*;
◆ at a lower price *(below par)* – to existing shareholders as rights issues;
◆ free *(bonus shares)* – to existing shareholders, usually in proportion to their existing holdings.

Comparative liquidity

It is almost always possible to sell shares given acceptance of the price offered. Share dealing occurs without the company's involvement and without any control or direction from it. There is no direct financial effect on a business from this share trading, except that future issues to raise further capital will be affected by both the current price and ownership of its shares.

Shareholders can only withdraw their capital by selling their shares

Only on business closure will this not be the case. On these occasions, shareholders will be paid out of the proceeds of company assets, once any creditors have been reimbursed.

Dividend payment

Dividends are the shareholders' annual income. The amount paid is based on net profits but is also at the directors' discretion. If some profits are retained, dividends will be reduced. Where profits are wholly retained, shareholders will receive no payout at all, but will (presumably) benefit in the long run from company growth and future profits.

Because of this discretionary element, the annual cost of share capital will vary. However, over the long term, the cost of ordinary shares will equal the rate of dividend which needs to be paid to maintain the market value of the company. This can be calculated as:

$$\text{Cost of ordinary share capital} = \frac{\text{Dividend per share} \times 100}{\text{Market value of share}}$$

Note, however, that this calculation assumes that all profit goes to dividend. If this is not the case and income is retained, it gets a little more complicated because part of the return to shareholders is in the form of capital growth, i.e. an increase in the real value of their investment in the company.

Preference shares

Preference shares carry less risk than ordinary shares since holders have preference in respect to dividend payments (a certain percentage must be paid, irrespective of profit) and on the wind-up of a company, when repayment of capital is made from residual assets. The only problem for preference shareholders is inflation, since returns are fixed in relation to nominal value and will therefore progressively reduce in real terms.

Cost to the business is similar to that of ordinary shares but there is not the complication of capital growth since preference share dividends and capital amounts are fixed.

Two further important considerations arise for companies wishing to raise share capital:

◆ Although the total number of shares on offer is limited only by existing authority and the state of the market, any increase will tend to dilute the original ownership.

◆ Since preference shareholders have preferred rights and less risk, companies will generally wish to restrict the proportion of these in relation to ordinary shares. Some companies, in fact, have no preference shareholders.

Costing finance

Since finance is itself a business resource, it is helpful if businesses know what its true cost is in relation to:

◆ other resources utilised during business activity (e.g. labour or materials);

◆ any alternative mix of finance source that might have been employed;

◆ the returns which may be attributed *directly* to it.

Average and marginal cost

Average cost is an important measure of overall business finance costs, whereas *marginal cost* will influence particular investment decisions.

We will take, as an example, a business already possessing a variety of existing loan capital, but wishing to raise further finance.

Existing loan capital:

Type of loan	£	% interest per annum
Debentures	50 000	8
Bank loan	15 000	12
Overdraft	5 000	15
Hire-purchase	20 000	20

Average cost = Total finance costs divided by total finance

$$= \frac{(50\ 000 \times 8) + (15\ 000 \times 12) + (5000 \times 15) + (20\ 000 \times 20)}{90\ 000} = 11.7\%$$

If the company can only borrow currently at 25 per cent (it has used up sources of lower cost finance), then *marginal cost* is also 25 per cent. Any project using new loan capital must therefore bring a correspondingly greater return if it is to be viable.

The ratio between average and marginal cost of finance will change as a business develops. At start-up, finance (especially low-cost forms) may be difficult to obtain. Marginal cost will usually fall relative to average cost with growth and increasing confidence, leading to easier access to low interest rates. In time, as these low-rate sources are used up, marginal cost will rise and eventually increase above average cost.

Capital structure

This is simply the mix of different types of capital employed by a business. One of the most important aspects of financial management is identifying and achieving an optimum mix. In a general sense, it is fairly easy to define the limits of any particular finance source. Share capital, for example, will be limited by market considerations and the need to restrict the number of preference shares issued. The penalties of fixed-rate finance, in a possibly volatile economy, may also restrict the take-up of sources such as debentures and fixed-rate loans, especially when interest rates are at high levels from the start. On the other hand, variable arrangements will always reflect the current cost of finance – for good or bad. Similarly, shorter-term bank loans, overdrafts and mortgages, as we have seen, all have their limitations and associated implications for the businesses making use of them.

Gearing

Financial managers need more precise ways of measuring these cost implications if they are to maintain a capital structure which is most beneficial to the overall (short-term and long-term) health of the company. The most important single measurement is that of the relationship between fixed-return and profit-related types of finance (equity). This ratio is termed *gearing*.

$$\text{Gearing ratio} \ = \ \frac{\text{Fixed return capital}}{\text{Ordinary share capital} + \text{Retained profit}}$$

Where this is below 1, the indication is of low gearing and consequently of a correspondingly low level of financial risk. The level of risk also depends upon profit volatility. If profits are stable, both highly geared and low-geared businesses will be at less risk than would otherwise be the case. Another qualification worth making is that a highly geared company may still have lower overall finance costs than companies in seemingly better financial health. This will happen where fixed rates are low and where the cost of share capital exceeds the cost of debt.

Interest cover

This is another measure of financial risk. If the interest cover ratio is low, interest payments are clearly a burden on profits.

$$\text{Interest cover} = \frac{\text{Profit}}{\text{Interest payments}}$$

MM theory

Named after its originators (US economists, Modigliani and Miller), this is an opposing view that the overall cost of capital is largely unaffected by capital structure provided the mix is not an extreme one. Capital structure is consequently irrelevant to any assessment of the value of the company, which is instead dependent upon commercial performance and risk – current and expected.

Whether or not this is true, in practice, financial managers are always going to try to avoid extremes of both equity or loan capital. The actual gearing ratio is probably less important than the need to accommodate the differing expectations of all types of investor.

Investment, return and risk

Here we are concerned, not with overall capital structure and cost, but with company decisions to invest in specific projects. These will carry varying degrees of risk and attract particular rates of return. Predictions of risk and return should consequently be made at the outset of each venture.

Capital investment

Business projects may involve capital expenditures on:

◆ equipment, e.g. the automation of a production process;

◆ new land or buildings;

◆ new production lines.

Investments of this nature are more significant to the long-term fortunes of the business than other expenditure decisions because they often involve:

◆ strategic implications, i.e. they will reflect and reinforce long-term aims and objectives as defined by the owners or managers of the company;

◆ long-term performance;

◆ large expenditures;

◆ significant increases or decreases in employment levels;

◆ increased training costs;

◆ opportunity costs related to the consequent inability to invest the same sum for interest;

◆ deferred returns;

◆ long-term effects on the levels of working capital required.

Investment appraisal

Capital investment decisions are consequently very important and fundamental, and will be taken at the highest levels within a company. Decision-makers will use experience and (possibly) intuition in their judgements, but they will also benefit from some form of investment appraisal analysis. There are a number of ways of calculating returns on capital investment. Let us examine just two of them here.

Average rate of return

If this is pre-set for a particular business project at, say, 20 per cent per annum, then the cost of any capital required to finance the venture may be offset against this figure. Provided the *average* rate of return over time is expected to exceed the cost of finance, a decision can be made to proceed.

For example, the cost and expected return of a project based on the acquisition of new industrial machinery which has an initial cost of £50 000 may be calculated as:

Required average rate of return	20% p.a.
Total cash inflow generated by the project	£100 000
Net inflow (gross income minus cost = 100 000 – 50 000)	£50 000
Net annual inflow (ten-year project term = 50 000/10)	£5 000

Since the initial investment was £50 000 but will have been fully repaid over the ten years out of increased income, the amount invested at the end of the ten years is nil. The *average* amount invested may therefore be reasonably calculated as half the initial cost. This is £25 000. We can consequently arrive at the average rate of return by calculating the net annual cash inflow as a percentage of this average amount invested:

$$\textbf{Average rate of return} = \frac{5000}{25\,000} \times 100 = 20\%$$

The expected returns have consequently been met and the project may be regarded as having been successful.

Payback

Unlike the average rate of return calculation, which emphasises overall profitability, this method concentrates on *early* payback of funds outlaid for a particular venture. A decision to go ahead will therefore involve adherence to some predefined minimum payback period. If this is set at four years, then, in our example:

Year	Net cash inflow (£)	
1	5 000	
2	8 000	
3	10 000	
4	15 000	
5	15 000	= £53 000 payback
6	15 000	
7	10 000	
8	10 000	
9	4 000	
10	8 000	(including residual value)

Payback is achieved in a little under five years, so the project would not go ahead under the set rule.

Payback is a simple method and is widely used. Providing their income predictions are more or less correct, companies employing it will rarely make bad investment decisions because of the inherent caution involved. On the other hand, since it favours early returns, losses may be incurred if profits (initially high) tail off rapidly to produce an overall deficit. In addition, the policy will tend to disfavour long-term investments, which, although in many cases may generate the largest overall profit, may also produce only small initial returns and even run at a loss for a period.

Other capital investment considerations

Working capital

In our example of the investment made in new industrial machinery and its associated returns, no mention was made of the additional costs likely to be incurred through an increased requirement for working capital as production grows. Where this is the case, the extra cost may be included as part of the initial investment. However, since the associated funds will be released at the end of the project, they may be included in the calculation of return as an additional inflow at the close.

Abandoned projects

If projects are abandoned before their expiry date, funds are again released, although, of course, associated income will also cease. In these cases, the residual value of any equipment purchased will be higher than anticipated. Consequently, as with working capital, this may again be included with the inflow realised during the final year.

Risk

It seems to be an inescapable feature of human life and behaviour that the reward for any action we may take is most often proportional to the degree of risk involved. Certainly this is true of investment decisions.

It is in the nature of risk that its assessment is only possible over time and if sufficient historical evidence becomes available. For example, insurance companies build their entire business on probability of risk. They can only do this through compilations of the statistical probability of each type of event, and through their own claims experience.

If the risk of being killed following a free fall from an aircraft is virtually 100 per cent, how might a company assess the risk associated with a venture, which (although similar to many others made by itself and others in the past) remains unique in its combination of local and external conditions, applying at a specific period of time?

One answer is to ignore risk completely on the grounds that some projects are good and some bad – so (overall) we will return x per cent come what may. Unfortunately, the assumed levelling-out process, while it undoubtedly does operate, would rarely be a sufficient basis for dealing with risk in business life. This is largely because the expectations associated with most projects exceed an average return, where this is calculated in relation to worst and best possible scenarios. For example, if it is theoretically possible for a project to return £1 000 000 at one extreme, and nothing at the other, it is unlikely its proposers will have split the difference in their forecasts. The tendency is to be optimistic and to predict average returns towards the higher end of the range of possibility, rather than the lower.

It is probably beneficial, therefore, for businesses to at least try to assess risk and to include this in their forecasts. Again, we will look at a couple of the methods that are employed.

Risk discounting

This is a very simple approach using experience gained from investing in similar projects. If this experience shows that, in the majority of cases, returns are 1 or 2 per cent below expectations, this discount rate can be added to the percentage annual cost of capital employed in any calculations made. The lower than forecast return has now been discounted before the project starts.

Sensitivity analysis

This is a more sophisticated and complex approach. It attempts to overcome the problem that the returns from a project are composed of not one but several different elements – each one of which may produce different results to forecasts, and may have a proportionately different effect on overall returns.

For example, assume project cost and return is predicted as:

			£	£
Sales revenue				200 000
Direct costs:	labour		80 000	
	materials		40 000	
	overheads	(fixed)	25 000	
		(variable)	15 000	160 000
Net inflow from project				40 000

These figures can be analysed to calculate how sensitive the overall net project income (£40 000) might be to any variance from forecast in each of the constituent elements.

Let us assume a variance of 5 per cent for each element.

Sales – selling price: Variance = 5% of £200 000 = £10 000

$$= \frac{10\ 000}{40\ 000} \times 100$$

= 25% impact on overall results

Sales – volume: Variance = 5% of Total net inflow + Fixed overheads
                        = 5% of (£40 000 + £25 000) = £3250

$$= \frac{3250}{40\ 000} \times 100$$
$$= 8\% \text{ impact}$$

Labour: Variance = 5% of £80 000 = £4000

$$= \frac{4000}{40\ 000} \times 100$$
$$= 10\% \text{ impact}$$

Materials: Variance = 5% of £40 000 = £2000

$$= \frac{2000}{40\ 000} \times 100$$
$$= 5\% \text{ impact}$$

Fixed overheads: Variance = 5% of £25 000 = £1250

$$= \frac{1250}{40\ 000} \times 100$$
$$= 3\% \text{ impact}$$

Variable overheads: Variance = 5% of £15 000 = £750

$$= \frac{750}{40\ 000} \times 100$$
$$= 1\% \text{ impact}$$

We can see from these calculations that this project is most sensitive to incorrect estimation of selling price (25 per cent effect on overall inflow).

Business planning

Although their accounting practices and legal requirements are relatively simple, start-up and small businesses are much less independent than their larger and more established counterparts. Much like the first-year student, they are consequently more inclined to follow rules, abide by set standards, and to try to satisfy the expectations of the banks and other agencies with which they have to deal. What they need is a business plan which:

◆ defines their ideas and objectives in realistic terms;
◆ quantifies their assets;
◆ assesses their non-financial resources;
◆ outlines their financial requirements;
◆ contains realistic forecasts of sales and cash flows;
◆ provides evidence of risk and future profitability.

Although there is no one standard format, the general structure is well known and almost any bank will provide a template and guidelines if this is requested. The most important elements are listed in Table 2.2.

Table 2.2   Start-up business plan structure

Business plan elements

◆ *The business*	Trading name and address Description Legal status and statutory requirements (sole trader, franchise, partnership or limited company)
◆ *The owner (s)*	Name and address Relevant experience and qualifications Personal goals and objectives Expectations and needs of other interested parties Survival budget Profit expectations SWOT analysis and training needs
◆ *Employees*	Experience, skills and qualifications Training requirements
◆ *The market*	Business idea Market research: – sources – current business climate – financial appraisal of the market – competitor analysis – target customers – customer needs and wants – product/service lifecycle – USP (unique selling point)
◆ *Resources*	Availability and cost of premises Equipment requirements (availability and cost) Material requirements (purchasing plan) Stock control Working capital requirements Assets and liabilities Total capital requirements
◆ *Pricing*	Pricing strategy and mechanism
◆ *Sales forecast and plan*	
◆ *Operating costs*	Direct costs Overheads Cash flow and breakeven

Summary

◆ We began by looking at different kinds of business organisation and associated legal status. Many incorporated businesses remain in private hands but the larger the company the more likely it is to have its shares on public issue. This brings advantages, especially in relation to raising finance, but there are also drawbacks.

◆ The commercial banks are important sources of short-term finance, but longer-term capital requirements are met by other forms of loan capital, such as debentures, and by share issues.

◆ The Stock Exchange is the focus for share and debenture dealing. Ordinary shares are profit-related investments, whereas preference shares attract fixed returns. Share capital may be raised from private investors and (more significantly) through financial institutions such as merchant banks, unit trusts, investment funds, pension funds and insurance companies.

◆ The main ways of raising business finance are:
   – bank loans and overdrafts;
   – hire purchase and leasing;
   – debentures;
   – retained earnings;
   – utilising current liabilities;
   – debt factoring;
   – ordinary share capital;
   – preference shares.

◆ These will possess different cost structures. Finance can be costed much as any other resource – the simplest measures being *average* and *marginal cost*. It is important for businesses to maintain a balanced capital structure. A simple measure of fixed-return to profit-related finance is the *gearing ratio*. Although there is a view (MM theory) that capital structure is not that significant, it is at least advisable for financial managers to avoid extremes by relying too heavily on one kind of finance.

◆ Capital investment decisions are strategic in nature and should be assisted by some form of investment appraisal. Average rate of return and payback approaches are simple and widely used in this respect.

◆ Risk may be ignored in the hope that levelling out will occur over time. However, companies often discount risk in their assessment of project viability by analysing probable outcomes with reference to previous experience.

Assignments

1 Choose a couple of high street banks which offer the full range of services to ordinary business account customers.

Compare their terms and costs in respect to:

◆ maintaining a business account;
◆ agreed overdrafts;
◆ non-agreed overdrafts;
◆ credit card;
◆ non-secured loans.

Summarise any differences you find.

2 Calculate the total cost (£) and average cost (%) of finance over one year for a small business customer of one of these banks, who has the following debts:

◆ agreed overdraft: £5000 (average = £3500);
◆ credit card: £1500 (average balance);
◆ unsecured loan: £7000 (five-year term).

3 A company requires that any new project can only proceed if *either*:

◆ forecast average rate of return is at least 18 per cent; *or*
◆ forecast payback period is no more than three years.

Will a project with an initial investment of £100 000 and forecast annual returns as set out below get the go-ahead?

Year	Forecast net return (£)
1	5 000
2	10 000
3	15 000
4	20 000
5	20 000
6	20 000
7	15 000
8	10 000
9	5 000
10	8 000

Case studies

Examine the following business scenarios.

1 Outline what you consider to be the most appropriate ways of financing the businesses or business projects described in the following sketches.

(a) Investigations agency

Partnership of two ex-police officers
Assets: Goodwill contacts with law firms
                   Homes valued at £80 000 and £100 000
Liabilities: Mortgages of £30 000 and £40 000
Requirements: Vehicles
                   Premises
                   Surveillance equipment (cameras, mobile phones)
                   Working capital

(b) Fast-food franchise

Unemployed man – some experience as a chef
Assets: None
Liabilities: None
Requirements: £10 000 to acquire franchise
                   £5000 working capital
                   Business training

(c) Greengrocers

Sole trading independent retailer. Business operating for five years.
Assets: Premises valued at £60 000
                   Delivery van value £5000
Liabilities: Mortgage of £30 000
                   Car loan of £5000
                   Overdraft of £1000
                   Credit card debts of £2500
Requirements: Expanded business and premises to increase income
                   Consolidation of debt for smaller repayments

(d) Premier League football club

Privately-owned. Small number of shareholders.
Assets: Stadium and practice facilities
                   Players
                   Catering and merchandising operations
                   TV and sponsorship deals
                   'goodwill' of fans
                   £5 m from recent transfer fees
Liabilities: Insignificant
Requirements: Bigger stadium and new sports complex
                   Additional players

2 If you were employed by a bank to assess applications for business loans and overdrafts, would you lend the bank's money to the following driving school venture? Give reasons for your decision – either way.

BUSINESS PLAN: CALM-WAY SCHOOL OF MOTORING

The business

Name:	Calm-Way School of Motoring
Description:	Driving School
Address:	12 The Way
	Waytown
Telephone:	Waytown 43434
Legal status:	Sole trader
	Sole proprietor

Licensing and authorisation:
Driving Standards Agency

The owner

Name:	Jed Calm
Address:	As business address

Technical skills and qualifications:
Clean, full driving licence
12 years' driving experience

Prior qualifications and experience:
GCE 'O' level passes in three subjects
10 years' experience as van driver
Redundant from last job at Waytown Supplies (3 years)
Previous jobs: Xway Supplies: 3 years
Yway Supplies: 4 years

Personal training needs:
Driving Standards Agency Approved Driving Instructor

Personal goal: To own and run a successful driving school

Financial needs:
Survival budget is £10 000 per annum
Expectations of profit in excess of this are £10 000 per annum

The market

Product description
◆ To provide quality, professional driving tuition.

◆ To provide a door-to-door service at all times of the day or week.

◆ To provide special programmes to fit individual circumstances.

Need for the product

Driving is becoming more difficult because of increased traffic. The driving test is now more demanding. Therefore, there will be an increase in the average number of lessons required. Waytown has a population of 18 000. There will always be a steady demand for driving tuition.

Competitors

Only three other schools are listed in Yellow Pages. These are:

◆ Betta-Bet;

◆ Sure-Bet;

◆ Each-Way Bet.

Only Sure-Bet has more than one car – it has three.

I also see competition from national schools but there are no offices in Waytown.

Target customers

◆ Sixth-form and college students.

◆ Women.

◆ Within 20 mile radius.

Financial appraisal

There is less unemployment and car sales are up.

Market mix

I did a telephone survey. The main points made were about previous results and price. If I kept the cost of lessons below £10 per hour and had a track record, I would get most of the business in the town – it seems.

The market mix is probably:

◆ product (tuition and pass) – 40 per cent;

◆ service (time and pick-up to suit) – 20 per cent;

◆ price – 40 per cent.

Resources

Premises

Private house. No significant costs incurred on buildings or furniture.

Contact with customers will be via telephone and answering machine.

Equipment required

Dual-control tuition car (Vauxhall Corsa, Ford Fiesta or Nissan Micra):

	Cost: £12 000	
Answering machine:	Cost:	£60
Mobile phone:	Cost:	£200

Capital requirements

Capital requirements:	£18 000 including working capital
Assets:	£1500 in building society savings account
Liabilities:	Credit card debt of £700
Financial assistance required:	Overdraft facility of £2000 for two years
	Business loan of £15 000

Pricing and costs

This will be based on what the market will stand:

◆ Basic hourly rate will be £12 for first six months.

◆ Discounts for special groups or block bookings.

Overheads		Earnings	
	£ per annum		*£ per annum*
Loan repayment	4000	Est. no. hrs of work per annum	2 000
Insurance	400	Less admin./travel time (20%)	400
Vehicle – running	2000		
depreciation	1500	Basic price per hour	12
Telephone	500	Annual earnings	19 200
Total (per annum)	8400	*Profit before tax*	10 800

Additional information

Sources of finance

Type of finance	Advantages	Disadvantages
Unsecured finance		
Owner's funds	Independence	100% risk
Friends, family	No, or low, interest Unsecured	Risk
Suppliers and customers	No, or low, interest Collaboration	Some loss of independence
Government and other grants	No, or low, interest	Have to submit detailed proposal and be within special categories
Unsecured bank loan	Easy to arrange	Interest Only small amounts, short-term

Type of finance	Advantages	Disadvantages
Overdraft	Easy to arrange	Interest Only small amounts May be called in by bank
Secured finance		
Leasing/hire purchase	Frees capital	Interest
Debt factoring	Frees capital	Interest Not available to small firms
Equity finance		
Individual investors or companies	Shared risk	Loss of control
Public issues	Shared risk Can raise large amounts	Dilution of control Only available to larger companies

Special help for start-up and small firms

Single Regeneration Budget	Government help for unemployed wishing to start in business. Administered by Training and Enterprise Councils (TECs) and Local Enterprise Companies (LECs).
Loan Guarantee Scheme	For small firms or individuals prevented from obtaining conventional loans through lack of security or track record. Guarantee is 70 per cent to 85 per cent on loans from £5000 to £250 000.
Regional Enterprise Grants Inner City Task Force Rural Development Commission	Various local assistance in depressed regions.
Prince's Youth Business Trust	Low interest loans to young people wishing to set up in business.
Enterprise Investment Scheme	Designed to help small unquoted businesses to raise share capital.

3 **Financial performance**

Learning objectives

◆ To describe the formats and conventions of:
  – the cash flow statement;
  – the balance sheet;
  – the profit and loss account.

◆ To identify the more common examples of subsidiary budgets.

◆ To recognise the main constituents of a basic set of company final accounts.

◆ To understand what is meant by the term inflation.

◆ To outline the effects of inflation on company accounting.

◆ To be aware of the main objectives behind the publishing of company annual reports.

◆ To calculate the main financial performance ratios and understand their relevance for business and financial management.

◆ To outline the factors involved in determining the amount of dividend to be paid to a company's shareholders.

◆ To understand basic approaches to placing a value on a business.

We have seen how companies manage their costs, how they generate income to create profit, and how they can arrange for proper levels and mixes of finance to be in place if their earnings are insufficient for investment requirements or where they are at a start-up point and need 'pump-priming' to get them on their way. In this chapter, we move on to the processes and methods by which businesses manage budgets, in particular how most of what goes on in a company ends up in some way being represented in the three basic financial statements that are familiar to almost all businesses. Finally, we will come to the more complex and more sophisticated financial reporting and analysis common to larger companies.

Basic financial statements

The three basic financial statements drawn from a business's internal budgeting process are:

◆ the cash flow statement;
◆ the balance sheet;
◆ the profit and loss account.

All three use the same information but interpret it in different ways and formats. The subsidiary budgets which feed into these are many and varied, and relate more specifically to the different functions and departments of a business such as production, sales, transport, wages, etc.

Cash flow

We have already seen that the cash flow forecast and statement records the quantities, origins and destinations of all cash movements into and out of a business. It is especially important for smaller businesses since it also produces a running balance of available working capital (*see* Table 3.1).

Balance sheet

Table 3.2 is a typical example of a balance sheet. It records (as either assets or liabilities) the balances of the different accounts held by a business. It therefore represents a business's overall financial strength and level of capital investment at the relevant date.

Table 3.1   Cash flow and working capital balances

Item	Apr £	May £	Jun £	Jul £	Aug £	Sep £	Oct £	Nov £	Dec £	Jan £	Feb £	Mar £
Sales/debtors	0	800	1000	1500	1500	1500	2500	4500	6500	1500	1000	1500
Capital	5000	0	0	0	0	0	0	0	0	0	0	0
Total receipts	5000	800	1000	1500	1500	1500	2500	4500	6500	1500	1000	1500
Drawings	1500	1500	1500	1500	1500	1500	1500	1500	1500	1500	1500	1500
Vehicle – running	100	100	100	100	100	100	100	100	100	100	100	100
Stationery	20	20	20	20	20	20	20	20	20	20	20	20
Telephone	200	0	0	200	0	0	200	0	0	200	0	0
Insurance	67	67	67	67	67	67	67	67	67	67	67	67
Total payments	1887	1687	1687	1887	1687	1687	1887	1687	1687	1887	1687	1687
Net in/ out	3113	−887	−687	−387	−187	−187	613	2813	4813	−387	−687	−187
Opening balance	0	3113	2226	1539	1152	965	778	1391	4204	9017	8630	7943
Closing balance (working capital)	3113	2226	1539	1152	965	778	1391	4204	9017	8630	7943	7756

Table 3.2   Balance sheet at 31 December

	£	£
Fixed assets		
Premises	70 000.00	
Machinery (at cost)	15 000.00	
Less depreciation	5 000.00	
		80 000.00
Current assets		
Stock and work in progress	50 000.00	
Debtors	15 000.00	
Cash	2 500.00	
		67 500.00
Current liabilities		
Creditors	15 000.00	
Overdraft	25 000.00	
		40 000.00
Working capital		27 500.00
Net assets		107 500.00
Financed by		
Capital balance (at 1 January)	80 000.00	
Profit	45 500.00	
	125 500.00	
Less drawings	18 000.00	
Capital balance (at 31 December)		107 500.00

Profit and loss account

This is a very important indicator of the commercial health of a company, and it may be useful to produce a profit and loss account at any time as required. It should at least be updated on a quarterly or half-yearly basis (*see* Table 3.3).

Table 3.3   Profit and loss account

	£		£	
Sales			50 000.00	100%
Purchases	32 000.00			
Opening	5 000.00			
	37 000.00			
Less closing stock	7 000.00	Cost of sales	30 000.00	60%
Less overheads:		Gross profit	20 000.00	40%
Premises	3 000.00			
Power	1 500.00			
Transport	1 200.00			
Telephone	600.00			
Depreciation	1 800.00			
Maintenance	800.00			
Insurance	300.00	Overheads	9 200.00	18.4%
Net profit before tax			10 800.00	21.6%

Notes:

Sales figures	= completed sales, i.e. for some sales, income may not yet have been received.
Purchases	= the difference between stock at the beginning and at the end of the period being covered.
Gross profit	= sales income minus direct costs.
Overheads	= all indirect costs.
Net profit	= income minus all costs (except tax).

Subsidiary budgets

Some examples are:

◆ sales, marketing and distribution costs;

◆ creditors;

◆ debtors;

◆ materials (costs, stock levels, turnover);

◆ finished goods;

◆ direct labour costs;

◆ buildings and maintenance;

◆ vehicles;

◆ utilities (heating, power, water, telecommunications, etc.);

◆ consultancy services;

◆ research and development;

◆ restructuring costs (e.g. redundancy payments).

In addition to being a statement of business activity and performance, any budget can provide the additional benefit of providing a set of criteria against which company objectives may be measured. It can also be used as a basis for analysing and assessing the comparative performance of the different functional components (or departments) of the business – a process which is further facilitated if the budgeting exercise is undertaken with the use of computerised spreadsheets, since the effects of any change to component figures is instantly seen. (We will look at some ideas and examples of spreadsheets later on in Chapters 4 and 5.)

A simple example of a departmental budget (*see* Table 3.4) illustrates how a department head (and the finance section) of a company can monitor and control expenditure by setting allocations for the year in each expenditure category, and then monitoring these as the year progresses. The objective should be to accomplish this without the excesses of over-centralisation (as was the case, for example, in the former Soviet-style economies of eastern Europe). Certainly, one of the reasons for the comparative economic failure of the Soviet Bloc seems to have been the stifling of initiative, innovation and local 'ownership' of economic activity through a concentration of decision-making power at the top.

Table 3.4   Departmental budget

Department: Computing							FY: 1996/97
Allocations:	Hardware	50 000.00			Expenditure:		37 600.00
	Software	10 000.00					7 050.00
	Consultants	5 000.00					470.00
	Maintenance	6 000.00					176.25
	Training	2 500.00					940.00
	Expenses	1 500.00					
		75 000.00		Cumulative	spend		46 236.25
				Balance			28 763.75

Item	Date	Supplier	Heading	Price	Quantity	Ex VAT	Inc VAT
Training	01/04/96	Trainix	Training	800.00	1	800.00	940.00
WizWord	30/05/96	Softinc	Software	150.00	20	3 000.00	3 525.00
Cheapo PCs	12/06/96	Chipper	Hardware	800.00	40	32 000.00	37 600.00
Stationery	30/07/96	Softinc	Consultants	5.00	15	75.00	88.13
Ink b/w	30/07/96	Softinc	Consultants	20.00	10	200.00	235.00
Ink colour	30/07/96	Softinc	Consultants	25.00	5	125.00	146.88
Repairs	12/08/96	Chipper	Maintenance	150.00	1	150.00	176.25
WizSheet	15/08/96	Softinc	Software	150.00	20	3 000.00	3 525.00

Final accounts

For limited companies (ltd and plc), the culmination of the budgeting process and its accompanying financial statements is the publication of final accounts. There is a legal requirement for these to be professionally audited.

Remember that the main difference between limited companies and non-incorporated businesses is that profits (or losses) belong to the company not to individuals. As such what happens to it must be recorded and be available for examination in the same way as are other aspects of a company's finances. The net profit is distributed (or retained) according to decisions made by directors. The actual distribution will be recorded in an *appropriation* section of the profit and loss account. This might be set out as in Table 3.5.

Table 3.5   Appropriation account (31 December 1996)

	£		£
Restructuring reserve	100 000	Balance at 1 January 1996	60 000
Computing reserve	20 000	Net profit to 31 December	195 000
General reserve	50 000		255 000
Preference dividend	15 000		
Ordinary dividend	50 000		
	235 000		
Balance c.f.	20 000		
	255 000		255 000
		Balance b.f. 1 January	20 000

There may be a number of reserve accounts like the ones listed here. For example, undistributed profit may be placed in a *revenue reserve*; an increase in fixed asset valuations may appear as a *capital reserve*; there may be reserves for future tax payments; and so on. They will all be represented in some form in the company's balance sheet. The larger and more complex the activities of a company are, the more the requirement for consolidation of the various accounts so as to provide shareholders with an overview of the company's year – as the example below shows.

IBM Consolidated Statement of Financial Position		(Dollars in millions)	
At December 31:		*1995*	*1994*
Assets			
Current assets:			
Cash		1 746	1 240
Cash equivalents		5 513	6 682
Marketable securities		442	2 632
Notes and accounts receivable – trade, net of allowances		16 450	14 018

IBM Consolidated Statement of Financial Position	(Dollars in millions)	
At December 31:	*1995*	*1994*
Sales-type leases receivable	5 961	6 351
Other accounts receivable	991	1 164
Inventories	6 323	6 334
Prepaid expenses and other current assets	3 265	2 917
Total current assets	40 691	41 338
Plant, rental machines and other property	43 981	44 820
Less: Accumulated depreciation	27 402	28 156
Plant, rental machines and other property – net	16 579	16 664
Software, less accumulated amortisation		
(1995, $11,276; 1994, $10,793)	2 419	2 963
Investments and sundry assets	20 603	20 126
Total assets	80 292	81 091
Liabilities and Stockholders' Equity		
Current liabilities:		
Taxes	2 634	1 771
Short-term debt	11 569	9 570
Accounts payable	4 511	3 778
Compensation and benefits	2 914	2 702
Deferred income	3 469	3 475
Other accrued expenses and liabilities	6 551	7 930
Total current liabilities	31 648	29 226
Long-term debt	10 060	12 548
Other liabilities	14 354	14 023
Deferred income taxes	1 807	1 881
Total liabilities	57 869	57 678

Source: IBM Financial Review 1995. Reproduced with permission of IBM Corporation.

The effects of inflation on company accounting

At the time of writing, the UK is experiencing a period of relatively stable prices and therefore of low inflation. It is easy to forget the effects of high inflation. In the UK, for a number of years in the 1970s and 1980s, the incentive to spend rather than save (despite relatively high interest rates) was so great that many people went on an unprecedented spending spree – especially in the housing market. The fear was that if your purchase was postponed for any length of time the price would rise more than any interest you might have received instead.

For those responsible for preparing business accounts, the main problems posed by inflation stem from the distortion of the base figures feeding into the accounting process, and of the forecasts which arise from it.

What is inflation?

Although inflation is most often measured as a percentage increase in the average price of goods or services, it is more accurately defined as a fall in the value of money (i.e. of sterling (£), the US dollar, or French franc, or of whatever the national currency that is affected). This is long-term movement – not the short-term ups and downs registered every day on the world's currency markets. Nor is it merely the price rises which affect only particular segments of the market or economy. It is a general upward trend in prices – as measured (in the UK) by the *Retail Price Index (RPI)*.

What we mean by long-term and what amount of inflation we consider to be taking us into an inflationary period depends upon our historical perspective. For example, in the United States, during the mid-1960s, an inflation rate of 3 per cent per year caused great concern, whereas the UK government has recently claimed victory over inflation by reducing it to between 2 and 3 per cent per annum. Furthermore, as the following newspaper article shows, if there are any signs of this figure being exceeded, the British government is placed under great pressure to act.

Clarke to deflate inflation fears as markets expect jittery week

Inflation figures this week will show prices rising at a rate well above the government's 2.5% target. But Kenneth Clarke, the Chancellor, will tell MPs tomorrow that inflation and interest rate fears are exaggerated.

November's retail prices index, to be published on Thursday, is expected to show little improvement on October, when the underlying rate jumped to 3.3%, and the headline rate rose to 2.7%.

With prices steady in November last year, a cut in the inflation rate will be hard to achieve, say officials, though a drop in the rate for December is expected.

After Friday's turmoil on world stock markets, analysts will be looking this week for indications of impending interest-rate hikes.

Remarks by the Bank of England governor, Eddie George, last week were taken by the markets to signal that the Bank would not be pushing for a base-rate rise this week.

Source: Sunday Times, 24 November 1996. © Times Newspapers Limited, 1996.

How do businesses account for inflation?

One way is to adjust figures to take account of the amount of inflation occurring between the date of a sale or purchase and the date of the particular financial statement involved. For example, if a company takes out a bank loan in January to create working capital, and then uses 50 per cent of the proceeds to acquire stock, any adjustment for inflation in end-of-year balances would need to take account of:

◆ any fall in the real value of the cash retained;

◆ any fall in the real value of the loan to be repaid;

◆ any rise in the value of retained stock dating from the January purchase.

This method is based on the purchasing power of money. The concentration is on cost at the time of actual purchase. Another approach is one which accepts that all materials (all resources) should be costed according to current, not historical, prices. Consequently, in place of the one-step historically based adjustment exercise, costs are *continually* adjusted according to current price. Since the adjustments are upwards, this will lead to the creation of a reserve fund which effectively increases the capital resources of the business.

 ## Company reports

The basic accounts of incorporated businesses (i.e. limited or public limited companies) are normally set out in an annual report. This will also include statements from the chairperson and chief executive, and contain specific information for shareholders concerning dividend distribution and retained earnings. Especially for the large national and multinational firms, these annual reports are becoming important vehicles for presenting and enhancing the company's status, objectives, values and image. Corporate image is an important commodity – worth the expense of professional logo designs, glossy publications, newspaper and television advertising and even Internet pages. Look, for example, at BT's 'Mission Statement', reproduced on the company's Web site (more on the Web in Chapter 5).

BT's mission, our central purpose, is to provide world-class telecommunications and information products and services, and to develop and exploit our networks, at home and overseas, so that we can:

◆ meet the requirements of our customers,
◆ sustain growth in the earnings of the group on behalf of our shareholders, and
◆ make a fitting contribution to the community in which we conduct our business.

Reproduced with permission of British Telecommunications plc.

 ## Financial performance ratios

In contrast to the detail of a modern company report, many aspects of business activity can be reduced to a single statistic (often a ratio or percentage) which provides an instant measure of performance in relation to:

◆ the perceived norm for business as a whole;

◆ the perceived norm for a particular business sector;

◆ historical values for the company concerned;

◆ forecast or planned values.

Before we have a look at the most significant of these measures, it is important to note some reservations. They tend, in particular, to give too short-term a perspective. One of the generally accepted problems of the UK economy is the short-term view of many investors. This can lead to pressure on businesses to produce high returns this year or next year. Companies may even be eager to maximise current year performance even though this goes against long-term interests. They know that good results impact favourably on shareholders, and upon the market in general, but that the effect soon wanes. If, on the other hand, results are poor, market patience will be tested and the company may have a difficult time raising further finance. Unfortunately, many expenditures which are charged against current trading do not produce returns for several years. Training is a good example – and again, in the UK, the relatively low training costs of industry have been frequently cited as a contributory cause of comparative economic decline in past years.

Of course, it is open to businesses to add riders and explanatory notes to reported performance figures. One of the more common features of company accounts over recent years, for example, has been the allowances made for restructuring costs or bad debt. (The example, shown below, of IBM's restructuring costs, reveals the extent to which such costs can reach, albeit for limited periods.)

Restructuring Actions

In 1993 and 1992, the company recorded restructuring charges of $8.9 billion before taxes ($8.0 billion after taxes or $14.02 per common share) and $11.6 billion before taxes ($8.3 billion after taxes or $14.51 per common share), respectively, as part of restructuring programs to streamline and reduce resources utilized in the business. As of December 31, 1995, the company had utilized all of the restructuring reserve balances except $225 million, which is necessary for actions that have been delayed into 1996.

Source: IBM Financial Review 1995. Reproduced with permission of IBM Corporation.

The more common ratios

$$\text{Average credit given (days)} = \frac{\text{Debtors}}{\text{Sales}} \times 365$$

$$\text{Average credit taken (days)} = \frac{\text{Trade creditors}}{\text{Purchases}} \times 365$$

These are simple measures of the extent of debt owed to suppliers or credit given to customers. Obviously, the lower the number of debtor days the better – conversely with creditors.

$$\text{Gross profit rate} = \frac{\text{Gross profit}}{\text{Sales}} \times 100\%$$

$$\text{Profit margin} = \frac{\text{Net Profit}}{\text{Sales}} \times 100\%$$

These are basic measures of commercial success and the higher the figure the better the business is performing in general. However, there are considerable differences between business sectors, with profit margins in some industries being generally much smaller than others. Volume car manufacturers, for example, tend to work on smaller margins than their equivalent producers of luxury cars, while retail margins can be as high as 40 per cent and more.

$$\text{Current ratio} = \frac{\text{Current assets}}{\text{Current liabilities}}$$

$$\text{Liquidity ratio} = \frac{\text{Liquid assets}}{\text{Current liabilities}}$$

These are measures of solvency. The general view is that both ratios should be at or a little above 1. If the ratios are low, cash flow is a problem. If they are high, capital is not earning, but sitting unproductively in a bank account.

$$\text{Stock turnover} = \frac{\text{Cost of sales (materials)}}{\text{Average stock}}$$

This is again relevant to the level and use of working capital. If turnover is high, stock is moving quickly and this is generally beneficial. If low, capital is again being tied up unproductively in excessive stock. The only exception to this would be in times of rapidly increasing stock prices.

$$\text{Return on capital employed} = \frac{\text{Net profit}}{\text{Average capital employed}}$$

This is perhaps the most basic indicator of commercial success. A favourable figure is high. However, it is important to note that these ratios are frequently misleading due to vagaries in calculating the underlying figures.

The shareholder's perspective

It is of course important not to forget the shareholder's point of view. Companies should be aware of their shareholders' requirements if they plan to stay in business. They know that individual shareholders (and the market in general) might be interested in any of the performance data outlined above. However, in the short term, they will be more concerned with actual dividend payments and share price.

Dividends

Dividends are paid from profits. These are defined as:

Realised profits – (Realised losses + Unrealised losses)

Realised in this context means that the profit or loss has actually occurred and has been accounted for. In the case of plcs, *unrealised* losses (i.e. losses incurred but not yet accounted for) must also be offset. These are legal constraints. In other respects, the amount of dividend paid is at the discretion of a company's directors. Although interim dividends are often paid during the year, decisions regarding final dividends will be made at the company's annual general meeting – and almost always carried, since shareholders may legally opt for a lower dividend but not a higher one.

There is an inherent conservatism involved in dividend distribution. This is mainly because most investors prefer a stable (and, hopefully, gradually rising) income. In addition, and reinforcing this, will be the directors' concern not to have widely fluctuating figures from year to year. A company which has an exceptionally good year and pays a large dividend may struggle to repeat the performance in the following year. If it does not, and the dividend payment is much lower, this may have an adverse effect on the company's status and value on the stock market.

The basic rule in calculating dividend is (or should be):

If retained income produces better returns than shareholders could get elsewhere, the business should retain the money. Otherwise it should pay out.

The proviso is that were a company to follow this rule unwaveringly, and as a consequence never pay a dividend, it would soon lose its ability to raise new share capital.

Let us look at some indicators especially concerned with shares and dividends.

$$\text{Earnings per share (EPS)} = \frac{\text{Net earnings}}{\text{No. of ordinary shares}}$$

This is a basic figure of earnings for each share.

From the EPS can be calculated:

$$\text{Share price : earnings ratio} = \frac{\text{Share price}}{\text{EPS}}$$

(High figures here are not necessarily bad since this may simply reflect market confidence and therefore a higher share price.)

$$\text{Dividend yield} = \frac{\text{Dividend}}{\text{Share price}} \times 100\%$$

This is the actual rate of return for each shareholder.)

$$\text{Dividend cover} = \frac{\text{EPS}}{\text{Dividend per share}}$$

(Any figure above 1 indicates that the company has retained some income.)

If we take BT as an example, the company's performance ratios are, as might be expected, very healthy. However, they do reveal a slight decline in profitability – almost certainly due to increased competition.

BT Financial Ratios year ended 31 March

	1992	1993	1994	1995	1996
Earnings per share – pence	33.2	19.8	28.5	27.8	31.6
Growth in net dividends per share %	8.3	8.3	7.1	6.0	5.6
Return on capital employed %	19.3	13.6	17.1	15.6	18.3
Gearing – net debt to equity %	21.1	14.3	9.3	17.8	7.4
Interest cover	11.1	9.4	13.0	10.3	18.2
Dividend cover	2.3	1.3	1.7	1.6	1.7

Return on capital employed

The group made a return of 18.3% on the average capital employed, on an historical cost basis, in its business in the year ended 31 March 1996, compared with a return of 15.6% in the previous year. The higher return is due to the lower level of redundancy costs in the year under review.

Earnings per share

BT's earnings of 31.6 pence per share for the year ended 31 March 1996 were 13.7% above the previous year's, principally because of lower redundancy and interest costs. The results have benefited from the strong growth in demand for BT's products and services and the improved efficiencies brought about by the redundancies of recent years, but the continuing impact of price reductions has offset much of these benefits.

Profit (1996)

	£m
Operating profit:	3 100
Group's share of profits of associated undertakings:	82
Profit on sale of group undertakings:	7
Profit before taxation:	3 019
Profit after taxation:	1 992
Profit for the financial year:	1 986
Earnings per share (pence):	31.6p

Source: British Telecommunications plc, Financial Review 1995/6.

Market value added/Economic value added (MVA/EVA)

This is a comparatively new kind of performance indicator, devised by American consultants Stern Stewart. It claims to remove any anomalies caused by differences in accounting practices, and to give a simple picture of whether shareholder's money has been 'created' or 'destroyed'.

The method is certainly simple. It takes the total capital invested in a company and subtracts from this the amount shareholders and creditors could take out of the business if they wanted. This leaves the *market value added (MVA)*. The MVA can be positive, which means that business managers have created money for their investors. Or, it can be negative, which means that investors' money has been destroyed. (There is a more detailed description of MVA/EVA linked with the case study at the end of this chapter.)

Valuing businesses

How much is a business worth? Performance figures are indicators of a company's value – not a valuation in themselves. If we define the value of a business in terms of its expected future returns, how are these to be calculated? Of course, they cannot be calculated precisely. In practice, a number of generalisations have to be made. What results is a valuation which should be greater than the value of current assets. For example, Kevin's garage business in *Coronation Street* is worth more than the value of its current assets only to the extent that there is a reasonable expectation of future profit. The difference is frequently quoted as that part of the price required to acquire a business which is above the valuation of its assets – paying for the 'business' or 'goodwill'.

Goodwill

MCI completed a significant acquisition of an information technology business in November 1995 for approximately $1,100 million. BT's share of goodwill arising on this acquisition is the main element of the £302 million written off to group reserves in the year, in line with BT's accounting policies.

Source: British Telecommunications plc, Financial Review 1995/6.

We know that existing shareholders are the prime target audience for published company accounts and reports, and that the significance of these reports is made all the greater because they have become such important ways of presenting corporate image, values and status. This significance is even further enhanced by a widely held belief among market analysts that a fundamental analysis of them can reveal a company's true (intrinsic) value. This is a valuation beyond that based on the current market price of its shares. It is inherent to the company, and, as such, will determine long-term performance. Now, if the stock market analyst can identify and quantify this intrinsic value before the market as a whole can work it out, the potential for gain is clear to see.

There is the alternative view which says that an analyst's opinion regarding a particular share price is irrelevant. The actual market price *is* the fair price since it represents the consensus. In this case, company accounts and reports, together with performance measures, take on less significance than a more general view of market prospects.

 ## Summary

◆ The three basic financial statements were identified as cash flow, balance sheet and profit and loss. These interpret broadly similar base figures in different ways to give an overall picture of the financial performance of a business. Subsidiary budgets relate to specific functions, activities or departments of a business. These feed into the main financial statements.

◆ Inflation can be a problem for the company accountant because it distorts base figures and can influence forecasts. It is accounted for by adjusting for historical changes, or through continual adjustments which lead to an inflation reserve fund.

◆ The basic accounts of large companies are included in published annual reports. These are increasingly geared to reflecting the status and projecting the image of the organisation to shareholders and the wider public.

◆ Many aspects of business activity can be quantified to produce financial performance ratios which can then act as criteria against which a company may be assessed. Unfortunately, these often reinforce the short-term views of the stock market and can encourage businesses to maximise current returns even where this is not necessarily in their best long-term interests.

◆ Dividend payments are largely at the discretion of company directors. On the whole, they adopt a cautious approach, fearing that expectations will be raised too much if particularly high dividends are paid in exceptionally good years. The tendency is to flatten out any volatility to give investors a regular, stable income.

◆ It is the view of some stock market analysts that a close examination of a company's accounts can reveal its intrinsic worth, and so its potential as an investment. The search is for companies which have a low share price relative to their potential, as estimated by the analysis. Others take the view that the market price of a share is always fair since it represents a consensus.

Assignments

1 Locate and read the annual reports of at least two large corporations.

Compare the reports under the following headings:

- company status and image;
- company objectives and values;
- profits and dividend.

2 How much (as a percentage) has the £ sterling fallen in value since:

- 1950;
- 1970;
- 1990?

3 List the financial performance ratios relevant to:

- solvency;
- overall commercial success;
- profits and dividend.

4 List the steps you might take to assess the value of a small business.

Case study

How useful is all this financial information? Can existing and potential shareholders spot a winner? Without any assumptions of investment expertise or any wish to ask you to play fantasy stock market, it might be interesting (and certainly instructive) to follow selected companies for 12 months to see what happens to an imaginary £1000 investment.

Use the article and survey, reproduced below, as a starting point. The survey selects 'winners' and 'losers', based on the market value added (MVA/EVA) analysis. Select from each category and do some research. You may not be able to undertake a fundamental analysis, but all the relevant information is publicly available and you will find that the more significant financial ratios are already calculated in respect to large plcs.

At the end of the 12-month period, what would have happened to your investment if it had been made in:

- a company from the top performers list;
- a company from the worst performers list;
- a bank or building society;
- National Savings?

Creating value: the best and the worst

MVA is a system of analysing performance devised by Stern Stewart, the American consultancy. Last year *The Sunday Times* published an MVA study of big British companies for the first time and today the results for 1996 are published, showing winners and losers, advancers and decliners among 200 top companies.

MVA strips out most anomalies created by accounting standards to paint a picture of whether a company has made or destroyed money for its shareholders. It gives a verdict on performance stretching back many years. The idea is simple. It takes the total capital entrusted to a management, adding up the money raised through share issues, borrowings and retained earnings. That gives a simple measure of how much money investors have poured into a company. It then takes the current value of the company's shares and debt, as a measure of what investors could take out of the business. The difference between the two is MVA, which measures how the executives have fared with the capital under their control. A positive MVA means that value has been created. A negative MVA means value has been destroyed. Plenty of adjustments have been made to published accounts, mainly on the capital side of the equation. It capitalises research spending and writes it off over a number of years. Two sectors have been excluded – financial services and utilities – mainly because it is difficult to compare these companies with those in other sectors.

The table ranks the 200 companies by MVA; the list is taken from a broader list of 500 UK quoted companies and the position of each company reflects its place in that ranking. It also compares each company's position with its position in 1995, allowing a judgement to be struck on whether a company is improving or declining.

(A related measure, the . . .) Economic Value Added (EVA), . . . takes each company's after-tax operating profit and compares it with its cost of capital. The cost of capital includes the cost of equity; what shareholders have an expectation of receiving through capital gains and dividends; as well as the cost of bonds and bank loans. The cost of capital varies for each company for two main reasons. Some businesses are more risky than others; investors will accept a lower return from a big food producer than from a high-technology start-up, because it is much more likely the food producer will generate stable returns. Secondly, companies vary their balance-sheet structures: some have more equity, which is more expensive; others rely more on cheaper debt.

The EVA figures represent the difference between profit and the cost of capital. The theory is that it is not good enough for a company just to make a profit. It has to make enough to justify the cost of its capital, equity included. If it is not covering that it will not make good returns for investors. Most conventional measures of performance, such as earnings per share, ignore the cost of the capital in a business.

So long as the return exceeds the cost of capital, the company can be judged to be adding value. Thus, if a company is generating EVA every year, over time its MVA should rise, and it should move up the table.

Joel Stern, of Stern Stewart, says: 'Board members still spend a lot of time talking about market share and growth, and not about delivering value to shareholders. They may talk about it, but there is a big difference between paying lip service to something and actually doing something about it.'

The list of MVA rankings certainly throws a radically different light on the performance of the companies. For example, BAT Industries, once described by Sir James Goldsmith as 'a machine for destroying value', turns out to be one of the consistently best companies at delivering value; it holds the number five slot it occupied last year, with an MVA of more than £11 billion. But Hanson, which built its philosophy around creating shareholder value, is the second-worst performer in the list, having a negative MVA of almost £2 billion.

The list, at the top, will confirm what many people suspect – that oil and drugs are the two global industries in which British companies excel. Those two sectors between them account for half of our top 10, taking in two oil companies – Shell and British Petroleum – and three drugs companies – Glaxo Wellcome, SmithKline Beecham and Zeneca.

But there are also two media companies in the top 10 – Reuters and BSkyB, which is 40% owned by News Corporation, parent company of *The Sunday Times*. Their presence suggests that Britain is creating leading players in the communications revolution.

Stern Stewart's research shows that relative positions in the table tend to be long term. Winning companies tend to keep on winning, losers keep on losing. Stern says: 'There is a lot of stickiness in the rankings, but you are not doomed to be at the bottom of the rankings forever. It is a matter of will, not of fate.'

The list does show the ability of some companies to make big moves rapidly. Hanson has moved down a long snake, but there are also plenty of examples of companies moving up a ladder as well.

Bass is among the more spectacular movers, rising from 488 last year to 38 this; Next is up from 358 to 64; BBA up from 216 to 88 and WPP up from 294 last year to 95 this. All have staged remarkable recoveries. But others are heading in the other direction. Rexam is down from 56 to 137; Northern Foods is down from 97 to 312 and Peninsular & Oriental is down from 48 to 462. British Gas has fallen spectacularly from 22 to 468.

Of the 500 companies in Stern Stewart's full list, 428 have a positive MVA. That is a worse record than in America, where just 59 of the top 1,000 companies have a negative MVA and even the biggest companies fall slightly behind their American counterparts.

Of our top businesses, only Shell would make it into the American top 10, at number six, between Microsoft and Johnson & Johnson. Glaxo Wellcome, our runner-up, would squeeze in at 11th place, just ahead of its drugs rival, Bristol-Myers Squibb, but somewhere behind the top American drugs company, Merck. However, our losses are not on the scale of those suffered by the Americans; British Steel does not have a negative MVA on the scale of Ford, RJR Nabisco or General Motors.

Companies that wish to improve their MVA may need to concentrate on actions and targets closely related to shareholder value creation, and align their pay policies accordingly, rather than rely on accounting measures such as earnings per share.

Three months ago the Burton stores chain started introducing EVA as a way of giving incentives to staff. John Hoerner, Burton's chief executive, says: 'The key benefit is to get people to realise that what

managers get paid for is making a return on the money in the company.'

In the past the company paid store managers bonuses based on sales, but that often encouraged them to order excessive stock, safe in the knowledge that if they could not sell it at full price, they could always dump it in a sale – a tactic that was good for turnover, and hence bonuses, but lousy for profits. The new system will force managers to think about how much capital they are tying up in their units and how they can lift the return on it.

So far, it has been introduced only for area managers, but will be pushed down to all shop managers in the next year. 'The senior people have always had to think about capital,' says Hoerner. 'But it is important that everyone in the company thinks about the cash they are using.'

Burton, which under Hoerner has jumped from 479th place to 62nd in a year, is not alone in adopting EVA. Other companies using or planning to introduce EVA systems include SmithKline Beecham and Barry Wehmiller International. Ultimately, the point of a company introducing EVA is to drive its MVA forward. Precise correlation on how well that works is hard to calculate, but common sense suggests that so long as a company keeps earning more than the cost of its capital it will be rewarded with a rising share price. And so long as its share price rises sufficiently, its MVA should go up as well.

No one measure can hope to capture the full story. There are criticisms to be made of MVA analysis. It is historical, a measure of track record rather than prospects, and is heavily influenced by the share price at the time the snapshot is taken.

That caveat aside, it has clear advantages. It strips away smokescreens thrown up by accounting conventions, and it allows investors to focus on real corporate returns. And it brings a simple idea to the fore: that managers should make more than the money put into their business costs. It may sound simple, but it is revealing how many big names fail to pass that test.

It also allows shareholder value to be more than a platitude. Next time a chairman talks about delivering superior returns, his audience will have a means of measuring how much his company has delivered in the past.

Source: Sunday Times, 8 December 1996. © Times Newspapers Limited, 1996.

200 UK quoted companies ranked by market value added (MVA)

Top 100 companies			Bottom 100 companies		
1996	*1995*		*1996*	*1995*	
1	1	Shell	103	88	Halma
2	2	Glaxo Wellcome	104	127	First Leisure
3	4	SmithKline Beecham	105	112	EuroTherm
4	3	Unilever	106	249	Medeva
5	5	BAT	108	69	Laporte
6	12	British Petroleum	109	114	Tate & Lyle
7	8	Reuters	110	129	Morgan Crucible
8	6	Marks & Spencer	111	111	Bunzl
9	10	BSkyB	114	123	Spirax Sarco
10	14	Zeneca	115		Mcbride
11	7	BTR	116	85	Christian Salvesen
12	13	Cable & Wireless	121	84	Kwik Save
13	11	Vodafone	123	360	Vickers
14	16	Guinness	124	158	Sema
15	23	EMI	127	205	MFI
16	9	BT	129	417	RJB Mining
17	17	RTZ	131	154	SKI
18	18	Grand Metropolitan	133		General Cable
19	15	Sainsbury	134	166	Greencore
20	20	Reed Elsevier	135	159	Beezer
21	26	GUS	136	164	Misys
22	21	Boots	137	56	Rexam
23	19	Vendôme	138	114	Waterford Wedgwood
24	28	Cadbury Schweppes	139	263	Ocean
25	27	Rentokil	141	118	TT
26	25	Tesco	145	96	Antofagasta
27	224	GEC	146	145	Telegraph
28	29	BOC	147	122	Amersham
29	34	Scottish & Newcastle	148	321	Cobham
30	31	Safeway	149	142	Low & Bonar
31	43	Siebe	151	102	Monument Oil / Gas
32	24	BAA	153	99	Croda
33	41	Reckitt & Colman	158	94	Rugby
34	50	Argos	160	78	NFC
35	42	British Airways	161	153	Cowie
36	100	Asda	165	300	Barratt
37	46	Granada	167	103	Glynwed International
38	488	Bass	169	131	Unichem
39	37	Pearson	171	117	Calor
40	32	Wolseley	172	104	Delta
41	35	Smith & Nephew	176	140	Hillsdown
42	115	Dixons	179	258	Independent News
43	52	Electrocomponents	180	87	English China Clays
45	72	Kingfisher	183	193	Flextech

Top 100 companies			Bottom 100 companies		
1996	*1995*		*1996*	*1995*	
46	75	Tomkins	187	194	Carlton
47	60	GKN	188	162	BTP
48	33	Williams	191	126	Ass British Ports
49	30	Allied Domecq	193	175	Trinity International
50	53	Hayes	200	169	House of Fraser
51	71	Smiths Industries	204	105	Booker
52	54	TI	211	138	Wassall
53	47	Burmah Castrol	214	221	Unigate
54	90	Ass British Foods	217	178	Fyffes
55	67	CRH	219	212	Scapa
56	191	Greenalls	220	198	Pentland
57	40	Enterprise Oil	222	213	Charter
58	68	Danka	224	124	Coats Viyella
59	59	Whitbread	238	108	Sears
60	81	Storehouse	242	277	Powell Duffryn
61	80	Compass	248	119	Airtours
62	479	Burton	256	237	Laird
63	133	Britis Biotech	271	453	Irish Permanent
64	358	Next	286	176	British Vita
65	73	Premier Farnell	301	223	Marley
66	57	Security Services	302	451	London International
67	86	Blue Circle	312	97	Northern Foods
68	79	Emap	333		Allbright & Wilson
69	49	Telewest Comms	381	428	Meyer International
70	58	RMC	384	172	Courtaulds Textiles
71	64	Elan	404	466	Baux
72	65	Chubb	423	409	Lex
73	93	Dalgety	430	318	Stakis
74	61	BPD Industries	453	414	Iceland
75	70	Daily Mail	461	484	Racal
76	55	Waste Man Intl	426	48	P&O
77	346	Cookson	465	116	BICC
78	89	Lonrho	466	471	Wickes
79	63	Securicor	468	22	British Gas
80	44	WH Smith	470	45	Inchcape
81	92	United News & Media	472	110	Redland
82	38	De la Rue	476	483	Amec
83	66	Morrison	477	486	George Wimpey
84	36	Jefferson Smurfit	478	470	Taylor Woodrow
85	149	ML Laboratories	481	473	Berisford
86	77	Allied Colloids	482	480	Rolls-Royce
87	95	Harrisons & Crosfield	483	490	Pilkington
88	216	BBA	484	485	Albert Fisher
89	76	IMI	486	229	Caradon
90	139	Bowthorpe	488	487	T & N

▶

Top 100 companies			Bottom 100 companies		
1996	*1995*		*1996*	*1995*	
91	496	Lasmo	489	493	Mirror Group
92	137	Kerry	490	481	Ladbroke
93	98	Stagecoach	491	101	Arjo Wiggins App'ton
94	51	United Biscuits	492	500	BAe
95	294	WPP	493	491	Tarmac
96		Nynex Cable	494	492	Cordiant
97	83	David S Smith	495	495	Sygnet
98	82	Hepworth	496	494	ICI
99	151	Matthew Clark	497	497	Trafalgar House
101	74	Johnson Matthey	499	135	Hanson
102	62	Courtaulds	500	498	British Steel

Source: Sunday Times, 8 December 1996/John Allen and Dianna Alvarez at Stern Stewart. © Times Newspapers Limited, 1996.

The 10 best sectors	*£m MVA*	The 10 worst sectors	*£m MVA*
Oil exploration & prod.	20 994	Health care	575
Pharmaceuticals	16 668	Leisure & hotels	553
Food manufacturers	8 814	Vehicle engineering	454
Telecommunications	4 388	Chemicals	379
Media	3 342	Building materials	342
Retailers	3 209	Distributors	300
Alcoholic beverages	2 948	Print, paper & packaging	211
Extractive industries	2 857	Engineering	170
Food retailers	2 347	Building & construction	27
Conglomerates	1 826	Gas distribution	–94

Source: Sunday Times, 8 December 1996. © Times Newspapers Limited, 1996.

4 Business statistics

Learning objectives

◆ To understand the need for sampling in statistical analysis.

◆ To recognise the differences between random and representative sampling techniques.

◆ To define and calculate the:
- mean;
- median;
- mode;
- standard deviation;
- normal distribution;
- binomial distribution.

◆ To outline ways of measuring change over time.

◆ To make appropriate use of absolute and relative cell references in computerised spreadsheets.

◆ To use simple mathematical and logical functions in a computerised spreadsheet.

◆ To recognise the benefits arising from the use of computerised spreadsheets in financial management and analysis.

We have seen how many aspects of business activity can be monitored through the use of specific types of statement, table or graph, and how snapshots of performance may be obtained by calculating a number of financial ratios which provide ready comparison with the company's historical progress, or with that of industry or the economy as a whole.

In this chapter, we take this mathematical approach to financial management a little further. In particular, the aim is for the reader to appreciate the usefulness of statistics and to see that, with an understanding of a few basic techniques, there need be no anxiety for even the least mathematical among us.

 ## Sampling and probability

Sampling

Imagine you are newly appointed to the financial management of a company. Your desk is a clutter of lists, schedules, inventories, reports, memos and financial statements. The paper on top of the pile highlights a serious problem of returned goods, possibly due to faulty bought-in components. No testing is carried out on site. Because of the large volumes involved, it would be prohibitively expensive to test all the supplies, which are obtained from a number of suppliers. The obvious solution is to take a sample of components and to test these. The results can then be taken to represent all of the supplied components (i.e. the *population* as a whole). How do you decide how many, and which items should be tested? There are two basic approaches.

Random sampling

This is, simply, sampling without any bias. For example, we trust that the UK's National Lottery numbers are selected randomly and without bias. Otherwise, not all tickets sold would have the same chance of winning. If we were to randomly sample our potentially faulty components, we would, first, need to know the size of the population. Let us say this is 10 000. We must now decide upon the size of our sample – say, 1 per cent. This means that 100 items are included in the sample. Individual components can now be selected by generating 100 random numbers in the range 1 to 10 000 (Table 4.1). These can be taken from a table or produced via a computer spreadsheet.

Unfortunately, this method requires that all items be numbered, more or less, consecutively. A simpler way is to select every one hundredth item. This is acceptable providing no pattern or structure is present in the population.

Table 4.1   Random sample

		Random numbers	Sample
Item 1*	Item 16	5	Item 1
Item 2	Item 17	10	Item 4
Item 3	Item 18*	4	Item 5
Item 4*	Item 19	22	Item 10
Item 5*	Item 20*	11	Item 11
Item 6	Item 21	26	Item 13
Item 7	Item 22*	1	Item 18
Item 8	Item 23	22	Item 20
Item 9	Item 24	13	Item 22
Item 10*	Item 25	20	Item 26
Item 11*	Item 26*	18	
Item 12	Item 27		
Item 13*	Item 28		
Item 14	Item 29		
Item 15	Item 30		

Representative sampling

If the population being sampled has an inherent structure, this should be reflected in the selections we make. In the case of our faulty components, there is no known structure or pattern. However, in our random sample, if a relatively large number of faulty components were to be identified with one particular supplier, we might bias future samples towards their products. In this case, a pattern is present which has caused us to create an unrepresentative sample.

It is much more common to attempt to create samples which are representative, and nowhere is this more common in business practice than in the areas of sales and marketing. If a business is aware that its market is predominantly composed of:

◆ males
◆ middle-income earners
◆ individuals aged 35–50
◆ home owners
◆ car owners
◆ readers of 'quality' newspapers
◆ subscribers to satellite or cable television

then , armed with this kind of information, sales and marketing managers can decide where and when to place advertising, and where marketing and sales activity and expenditure is likely to reap the greatest rewards. (The market, in this example, would presumably be relatively receptive to new consumer electronic products, such as wide-screen digital television or mobile phones, but be less interested in products geared towards a younger population, such as fashion accessories or popular music.)

Probability

If a 1 per cent sample of any population is truly representative, it is possible to estimate with confidence for the population as a whole. Opinion polls, for instance, regularly predict (from samples of little more than one thousand voters) the outcome of a general election, if it were to be held on the same day the opinion poll was taken.

The results of major opinion polls are usually accepted with a high degree of confidence (a plus or minus 3 per cent *sampling* error is often quoted). This is because the structure of the UK electorate (age, sex, socioeconomic factors, etc.) is known in great detail, as is their previous voting behaviour. In most cases, however, much less is known.

Let us go back to our faulty component problem. Another way of approaching it would be to measure the *probability* of a fault occurring in the given population of components. If no testing has been done, we can still measure probability from past experience. For example, we might reasonably estimate a 3 per cent failure in one range of components and 1 per cent in another because this is what has happened in the past. If testing is carried out, and we have a sample basis for calculation, it is then possible to measure probability through observation. If, in our test sample of 100 items (1 per cent of the total population), the actual failure rate is two, then our estimate for the total population would be:

$$\frac{2}{100} = 0.02 \qquad \text{therefore the probability is } 0.02\% \text{ of } 10\,000 = 200$$

Estimates of probability increase in accuracy with the number of tests carried out. A sample of 1 per cent would not carry the same degree of confidence as one based on a 10 per cent sample. In the National Lottery, the probability of any one number being drawn each week seems sometimes to be greater than chance, but this is only because we tend to view on a short timescale. Over the long term (and over many draws) its occurrence will settle to a level closer and closer to that of all the other numbers in the draw. Even over as short a timescale as five weeks (Table 4.2), the laws of probability seem to be operating reasonably well.

In these situations, where all different outcomes are equally likely to occur, it is possible to calculate probability in advance. Probability, in this sense, is based on the number of times a particular outcome *should* occur.

Table 4.2   Results of lottery draw over five weeks

Draw							Frequency		
12	24	33	34	42	47	(44)	1 (1)	22 (1)	46 (1)
							4 (1)	24 (1)	47 (2)
6	13	17	22	42	47	(30)	5 (2)	25 (1)	49 (2)
							6 (1)	26 (1)	
4	5	12	25	26	49	(48)	12 (2)	33 (2)	
							13 (1)	34 (2)	
16	33	34	43	46	49	(47)	16 (1)	37 (1)	
							17 (1)	42 (3)	
1	5	16	18	37	42	(24)	18 (1)	43 (1)	

In the deadly 'game' of 'Russian Roulette', for example, the probability that the participant will shoot himself is:

impossible	0%		– the gun is not loaded.
↑	16%		– one chamber of six is loaded.
↓	50%	(evens)	– three chambers are loaded.
certain	100%		– all six chambers are loaded.

The distribution of probability

If we are to make confident estimates for a total population based only on a sample of its data, we need to be aware of certain mathematical concepts which underlie the process. Those with which we are most familiar are the *mean*, the *median* and the *mode*. When these are calculated for any set of data, it is possible to see how the elements of the set are either concentrated around these *average* values or dispersed from them. This dispersal, or *deviation*, from average values can also be measured – as the *standard deviation*. We will also look briefly, here, at two common distributions of values which occur in many different types of data-set. These are the *normal distribution* and the *binomial distribution*. Both have general significance in many kinds of statistical analysis.

The mean

Commonly termed the average, this is the sum of all the numbers in a set divided by the number of elements in the set. For example:

In the set: (23, 32, 45, 12, 50, 26, 88, 67, 33, 97) the mean = 473/10 = 47.3

The median

This is the number in a set in relation to which, if the elements are arranged in order of size, half are larger and half are smaller. In other words the median is the mid-point. If the number of elements in the set is even, the median is taken to be the mean of the two mid-point numbers. For example:

In the set: (12, 24, 34, 36, 44, 57, 88, 93, 99) the mode = 44
In the set: (12, 24, 34, 36, 44, 57, 88, 89, 93, 99) the mode = (44 + 57)/2 = 50.5

The mode

This is the number in a set which occurs most frequently. There is no mode for a set in which all the numbers are different. If the most frequently occurring number is matched by another in the set, both are modes.

Standard deviation

We will see later how easy it is to work out standard deviation if we are assisted by a computer. For now, let us just define standard deviation as a useful measure of the spread, or dispersion, of a set of data about its mean value. It can be especially useful since it qualifies the mean. The latter sometimes gives an erroneous impression of data. For example (looking at the extremes), the means of both the following data sets are the same. However, the differences are highlighted by different values for standard deviation.

(15, 15, 15, 15, 15, 15, 15, 15, 15, 15): mean = 15
standard deviation = 0 (i.e. none)

(1, 1, 1, 1, 1, 1, 1, 1, 1, 141): mean value = 15
standard deviation = 44.27 (i.e. high)

Normal distribution

This is the distribution of values which, when depicted as a frequency curve, results in the characteristic bell-shape known as a normal curve (*see* Fig. 4.1). This means that if all the elements in a set are plotted either side of the mean value, more than two-thirds of them will fall within plus or minus one standard deviation from it. It follows that, given a normal distribution, the mean value provides a good prediction of the set as a whole.

Many sets of data have a normal distribution. For example:

◆ *measures of intelligence and educational attainment* – more people get C grades than get A grades or fail;
◆ *errors made in repeated, routine tasks and observations* – these tend to be just above or below (left or right) of what is correct, and therefore average out;
◆ *biological characteristics, such as weight or height of individuals* – if not, there would be equal numbers of men, six feet four tall as those five feet ten.

Sometimes data which is apparently not normally distributed when small samples are taken become approximately normal when the volume of data tested becomes large enough.

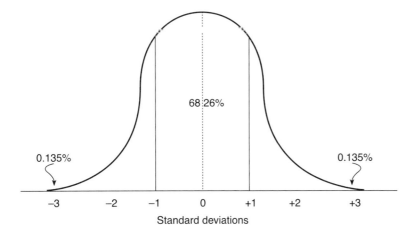

Fig 4.1 Normal distribution

Binomial distribution

This type of distribution describes the possible number of times that a particular result will occur in a sequence. If the probability of this result occurring in any one observation is known, the binomial distribution predicts the probability of the result being repeated in future observations. The obvious example here is that of tossing a coin. What is the probability of tossing 'heads' when a coin is tossed *x* number of times?

Number of heads	Probability	(x = 16)
0	1 in 16	1
1	4 in 16	4
2	6 in 16	6
3	4 in 16	4
4	1 in 16	1

In other words, in a sequence of 16 trials, you will probably toss heads three times in four tosses.

Time series

Much of the data used by business and financial managers is time related. Sales, income and profits are all variables likely to change over the long term and, in some cases, also over the short term.

We will take lager sales as an example. What factors influence sales over time?

◆ *Seasonal factors*. These are short-term influences. More lager is sold at the week-end than during the earlier part of the week. More is sold on hot days than cold days. More is sold at Christmas than in January and February.

◆ *Trend*. This is long term. There may be:

– no change at all;

– a constant rise;

– a constant fall.

◆ *Cyclical movements*. This is also long term but here there is no constancy. The movement is a swing upwards and downwards depending on general economic factors.

◆ *Random events*. These are unpredictable factors which may cause temporary blips or, perhaps, have a more long-term influence. For example, a health scare which linked lager drinking with premature baldness might put the brake on sales for a while.

Moving average

Now, while businesses might ignore cyclical and random factors on the grounds they can do little about them, it is often important to isolate the longer-term trends from any seasonal influences. A simple way of smoothing out short-term fluctuations is to calculate a *moving average*. In the example in Table 4.3, we collect sales figures over a number of days and then move a seven-day 'week' window through them, taking the average sales as we go along.

Table 4.3 Lager sales – moving average

Day	Sales (000 litres)		Moving average
Monday	300	(300 + 315 + 310 + 356 + 530 + 512 + 401)/7=	389
Tuesday	315	(315 + 310 + 356 + 530 + 512 + 401 + 320)/7=	392
Wednesday	310	(310 + 356 + 530 + 512 + 401 + 320 + 356)/7=	398
Thursday	356	(356 + 530 + 512 + 401 + 320 + 356 + 349)/7=	403
Friday	530	(530 + 512 + 401 + 320 + 356 + 349 + 360)/7=	404
Saturday	512	(512 + 401 + 320 + 356 + 349 + 360 + 554)/7=	407
Sunday	401		
Monday	320		
Tuesday	356		
Wednesday	349		
Thursday	360		
Friday	554		

If we plot these moving averages against the actual sales figures, a long-term gradual upward trend can be discerned (*see* Fig. 4.2).

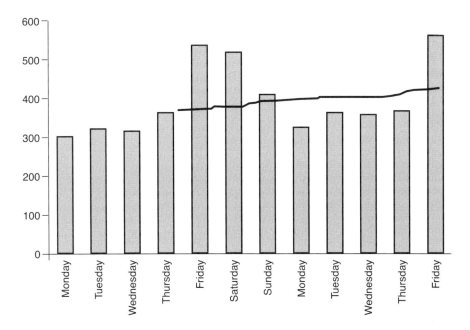

Fig 4.2   Lager sales (000 litres): moving average and trend

 ## Stock control

In Chapter 1, we saw the importance of maintaining optimum stock levels so that working capital was not tied up unnecessarily and unproductively. One of the important calculations in this respect is to define at what level stock should be reordered to ensure this while also maintaining sufficient for production. This is the *economic order quantity (EOQ)*.

Economic order quantity

We have to assume in working out EOQ that all the costs are known in advance and that we can predict with certainty what the delivery times and rates of consumption are. If we are to minimise stock, new supplies should be arriving as existing stock is just about exhausted.

If we define:

Q = our reorder quantity
H = the cost of holding one unit of stock for one year
A = administrative and other costs associated with placing each order
N = number of units of stock consumed each year

We then have:

Minimum stock = 0
Maximum stock = Q
Average stock = Q/2 (assumes that stock is consumed evenly)
Number of orders placed per annum = N/Q
Annual ordering cost = AN/Q
Annual holding cost = HQ/2

There are consequently two costs involved. Holding cost (HQ/2) decreases when frequent orders are made. Ordering cost (AN/Q) decreases when the ordering frequency is low.

Since one cost rises as the other falls, there must be some value of Q at which the combined costs are at a minimum. This is the EOQ. It is calculated as:

$$\text{EOQ} = \sqrt{(2AN/H)}$$

For example:

Annual consumption (N)	= 10 000
Holding cost (H)	= 50 pence per box
Ordering cost (A)	= £20 per order
Economic order quantity (EOQ)	= $\sqrt{(2AN/H)}$
	= $\sqrt{(2 \times 20 \times 10\ 000\ /\ 0.5)}$
	= 894 boxes

(We will add more detail to this example a little later on when we come back to it as a problem ideally suited to solution by spreadsheet.)

Using spreadsheets for statistical analysis

We will get to a more general discussion of the main features and capabilities of computerised spreadsheets in Chapter 5, where the focus will be on the information technologies which assist business and financial management. For now, let us look at the spreadsheet as a simple but much more powerful substitute for the calculator, pen and paper.

What follows assumes a knowledge of spreadsheet basics, such as:

◆ basic menus, getting help, etc.;
◆ how to load and save files;
◆ entering text and numbers;
◆ moving around the spreadsheet;
◆ copying and deleting cells, rows and columns.

If you do not know how to carry out these basic operations on some form of computerised spreadsheet then get someone to show you. Their use is pretty well essential nowadays for any business or financial manager or analyst.

Referencing spreadsheet cells

Relative cell references

A cell reference such as D2=B2*C2 is relative because it tells the spreadsheet program where to locate a cell relative to the starting location. Since the same calculation is repeated for each row (with only the row number changing), the relative reference causes the spreadsheet program to refer to D2 each time it moves down a row, and to add one to the row number. There is no change to the column letter because the calculation has remained in the same column. In this case, we wish the row numbers to change to calculate each cost in turn.

	A	B	C	D	E
1	Item	Price	Quantity	Cost	
2	Discs	£0.50	£200.00	£100.00	=+B2*C2
3	Paper	£5.00	£20.00	£100.00	=+B3*C3
4	Ink	£15.00	£30.00	£450.00	=+B4*C4
5	Toner	£30.00	£10.00	£300.00	=+B5*C5
6					
7					

D2=B2*C2

This is price times quantity for discs. We want this repeated for the other rows. If we copy the formula in D2 to D3, D4 and D5 the spreadsheet automatically adjusts for rows.

Absolute cell references

An absolute cell reference is one in which the exact original location (column and row) is used. In this example, we wish to apply VAT to the cost of each item. Since VAT is a constant value (17.5 per cent) we can enter this in a separate cell and use this in our formulae, which, no matter where they are copied to, retain the same cell reference.

	A	B	C	D	E	F	G
1	Item	Price	Quantity	Cost		VAT:	17.50%
2	Discs	£0.50	£200.00	£100.00	=+B2*C2	£17.50	
3	Paper	£5.00	£20.00	£100.00	=+B3*C3	£17.50	
4	Ink	£15.00	£30.00	£450.00	=+B4*C4	£78.75	
5	Toner	£30.00	£10.00	£300.00	=+B5*C5	£52.50	
6							

=+D2*$G$1

=+D5*$G$1

The dollar sign preceding both the column and row numbers keeps these constant in any formula referencing cell G1.

Mixed references

Sometimes it is convenient to use a relative column reference with an absolute row reference – or an absolute column reference with a relative row reference.

In the following example (p. 85), we wish to apply each discount rate to Item 1's full price by copying the formula +H2–(H2*A3) down to relate to each discount rate in turn. Since we wish rows but not columns to change from A3, we make the column absolute and the row relative: $A3. H2 contains the full price of Item 1 – which is a constant. Therefore, we need to have absolute references for both row and column in this case: $H$2. Similarly, references to H3 and H4 are also absolute.

Names

The spreadsheets and formulae that we have looked at so far are relatively straight-forward ones, and yet, already, it is becoming difficult to remember cell references and to relate particular cells to particular variables. However, if a cell contains a discount percentage or a VAT rate, it can be named *Discount* or *VAT*, respectively. It is much easier to understand a formula if its elements contain meaningful names such as VAT rather than G1. Ranges of cells, columns and rows can also be given names. For example, if a certain part of a spreadsheet contains summaries of values calculated elsewhere, it might be convenient to name this range, *Summary*. It can then be referred to more naturally while navigating around a large spreadsheet. (Naming procedures vary slightly between different spreadsheet programs so we won't detail them here.)

	A	B	C	D	E	F	G	H	I
1	Discount			Discounted price				Full price	
2			Item 1	Item 2	Item 3		Item 1	£100.00	
3	0.05		95	190	285		Item 2	£200.00	
4	0.1		90	180	270		Item 3	£300.00	
5	0.2		80	160	240				
6	0.25		75	150	225				
7	0.3		70	140	210		absolute	reference	
8	0.35		65	130	195				
9	0.4		60	120	180		mixed	reference	
10									

```
=+$H$2-($H$2*$A3)        =+$H$3-($H$3*$A3)        =+$H$4-($H$4*$A3)
=+$H$2-($H$2*$A4)        =+$H$3-($H$3*$A4)        =+$H$4-($H$4*$A4)
=+$H$2-($H$2*$A5)        =+$H$3-($H$3*$A5)        =+$H$4-($H$4*$A5)
=+$H$2-($H$2*$A6)        =+$H$3-($H$3*$A6)        =+$H$4-($H$4*$A6)
=+$H$2-($H$2*$A7)        =+$H$3-($H$3*$A7)        =+$H$4-($H$4*$A7)
=+$H$2-($H$2*$A8)        =+$H$3-($H$3*$A8)        =+$H$4-($H$4*$A8)
=+$H$2-($H$2*$A9)        =+$H$3-($H$3*$A9)        =+$H$4-($H$4*$A9)
```

Spreadsheet functions

All spreadsheets have built-in mathematical and logical functions which make the task of analysing numerical data much easier than is the case with manual calculation. We will look at a few common ones here and list some of those which are particularly useful for financial analysis. We will then revisit our economic order quantity (EOQ) calculation and example of standard deviation to see how easy it is to do the calculations and build simple spreadsheets which are practical aids to financial planning and cost management.

SUM(   )   Sums a range of cell values

The range is defined as the first and last cells separated by a dot. In all modern systems, this is an automated function which can be selected from a toolbar.

	A
1	
2	45
3	32
4	125
5	453
6	23
7	4
8	56
9	SUM(C2.C8) = 738
10	

STDEV(   ) Calculates the standard deviation from the mean

Refer back to the example of age distribution and the sometimes misleading calculation of the mean. The two sets of ages given were extremes:

(15, 15, 15, 15, 15, 15, 15, 15, 15, 15): mean value = 15
standard deviation = 0 (i.e. none)

(1, 1, 1, 1, 1, 1, 1, 1, 1, 141): mean value = 15
standard deviation = 44.27 (i.e. high)

A more realistic sample might give:

(35, 37, 55, 34, 46, 55, 32, 54, 45, 51)

If we enter these in a spreadsheet we can give them a name *ages*, apply the function and the standard deviation is calculated for us.

	A	B	C	D	E	F	G	H	I	J	
1	35	37	55	34	46	55	32	54	45	51	range name = ages
2											STDEV(ages) = 9.24
3											AVERAGE(ages) = 44.4

If (   ) Sets up a condition which, if true, executes one action or, if false, executes an alternative action

This is a bit more complex, but it sets up all sorts of possibilities for selecting out

	A	B	C
1	Age		Pension payable?
2			
3	14		0
4	16		0
5	66		1
6	45		0
7	23		0
8	12		0
9	56		0
10	67		1
11	76		1
12	43		0

= IF(A3>64,1,0)

IF(condition, TRUE action, FALSE action). If the values in column A are over 64 place 1 in the cell, otherwise (i.e. FALSE) place zero in the cell.

Common functions

Those listed here are available in Microsoft's Excel 5 spreadsheet. Other systems may vary (although only slightly) from Microsoft's naming conventions.

Statistical

AVERAGE	Returns the average of its arguments
COUNT	Counts how many numbers are in the list of arguments
LARGE	Returns the largest value in a data set
MAX	Returns the maximum value in a list of arguments
MEDIAN	Returns the median of the given numbers
MIN	Returns the minimum value in a list of arguments
MODE	Returns the most common value in a data set
RANK	Returns the rank of a number in a list of numbers
SMALL	Returns the smallest value in a data set

Logical

AND	Returns TRUE if all its arguments are TRUE
FALSE	Returns the logical value FALSE
IF	Specifies a logical test to perform
NOT	Reverses the logic of its argument
OR	Returns TRUE if any argument is TRUE
TRUE	Returns the logical value TRUE

Mathematical and statistical functions

RAND	Returns a random number between 0 and 1
SQRT	Returns a positive square root
STDEV	Returns the standard deviation
SUM	Adds its arguments

Mathematical operators

+	Addition		−	Subtraction
/	Division		*	Multiplication
%	Per cent		=	Equal to
>	Greater than		<	Less than
>=	Greater than or equal to		<=	Less than or equal to
<>	Not equal to			

A spreadsheet solution

We can now revisit the EOQ calculation. The figures were:

$$\text{EOQ} = \sqrt{(2AN/H)}$$

Annual consumption (N) = 10 000
Holding cost (H) = 50 pence per box
Ordering cost (A) = £20 per order
Economic order quantity (EOQ) $= \sqrt{(2AN/H)}$
$= \sqrt{(2 \times 20 \times 10\,000/0.5)}$
$= 894$ boxes

If we enter these on a spreadsheet, the main advantage is not that we can now use the program's square root function (convenient though this is). The real gain is the ability to widen the scope of the analysis, and to see, immediately, the effects of any changes to any of the figures. It would be nice, for example, to be able to verify the result of 894 and to see what effect on overall stock costs different ordering quantities would have.

The constant values are first entered onto the spreadsheet, and then referenced to the calculations which follow.

	A	B	C	D
1	Annual consumption (N) =	£10,000.00		
2	Holding cost per box (H) =	£0.50		
3	Ordering cost per order (A) =	£20.00		
4	Economic order quantity (EOQ) =	$\sqrt{(2AN/H)}$ $=\sqrt{(2 \times 20 \times 10{,}000/0.5)}$	= SQRT((2AN/H)) = 894	
5				
6				
7	No. boxes	Holding cost	Order cost	Total stock costs
8				
9	500	£125.00	£400.00	£525.00
10	894	£223.50	£223.71	£447.21
11	1000	£250.00	£200.00	£450.00
12	2000	£500.00	£100.00	£600.00
13	4000	£1,000.00	£50.00	£1,050.00

No. boxes	Holding cost	Order cost	Total stock costs
500	=+$C$2*B9/2	=+$C$3*$C$1/B9	=+B9+C9
894	=+$C$2*B10/2	=+$C$3*$C$1/B10	=+B10+C10
1000	=+$C$2*B11/2	=+$C$3*$C$1/B11	=+B11+C11
2000	=+$C$2*B12/2	=+$C$3*$C$1/B12	=+B12+C12
4000	=+$C$2*B13/2	=+$C$3*$C$1/B13	=+B13+C13

Let me provide a little more explanation. Constant values are placed in cells C1, C2 and C3. These could just as easily have been named as: *consumption, holding_cost* and *order_cost* respectively, and referred to as such in the formula. The economic order quantity (EOQ), we already know, is the square root of two times the annual order cost divided by the holding cost ($\sqrt{2AN/H}$). In Microsoft Excel, the square root function is SQRT( ). The formula is therefore SQRT(2AN/H). Using our figures from the earlier example, this translates as: SQRT(2 × 20 × 10 000 / 0.5), which comes to 894. The spreadsheet then allows us to verify this figure and see the effect on costs of different ordering practice. We need to use absolute cell references for the constant values so that these won't change when we copy formula. Otherwise, the references are relative and allow us to repeat the calculation of cost for the different order amounts. The effect of increasing holding costs but decreasing order costs as order amounts rise is clearly seen.

Finally, let us see how easy it is to turn the results into a graph. Figure 4.3 was created with a few mouse clicks.

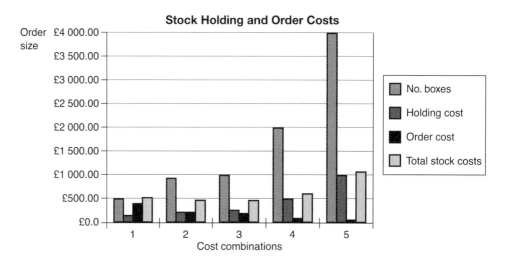

Fig 4.3   Graphing spreadsheet results

 ## Summary

◆ All kinds of statistical analysis are based on sampling techniques and on the rules of probability. Some samples are compiled on a random basis, others use some form of structuring to make them as representative as possible.

◆ Any numerical data set can be described in terms of its:

– mean;

– median;

– mode.

◆ Many data sets have a *normal distribution* of values around the mean. This means that more than two-thirds of the constituent values fall within plus or minus one *standard deviation* from the mean.

◆ A *binomial distribution* describes the probable number of times that a particular result will occur in a given sequence of possible results.

◆ In time-based analyses, the objective is to isolate long-term trends from short-term fluctuations and from random events. One technique is to calculate a *moving average* to smooth out the ups and downs.

◆ Stock holding costs can be minimised by calculating an *economic order quantity*. This and many other examples of financial analysis are made much easier by the use of computerised spreadsheets, most of which include a range of mathematical, statistical, financial and logical functions.

Assignments

1 How would you set about constructing a representative sample for a survey of political opinion?

2 If you have access to a computer, find out how to generate a set of 20 random numbers between 1 and 500.

3 Toss a coin 16 times. Does the number of heads tossed equate with a binomial distribution of probability?

4 Find out how many times base interest rates have changed since the 1992 general election. What has been the trend since then?

5 If you have access to a computer and spreadsheet program, enter the following data set, calculate the mean and create a graph to depict monthly variation.

Month	Average temperature (°C)
January	4
February	6
March	9
April	12
May	15
June	19
July	23
August	22
September	18
October	14
November	9
December	5

Case study

Construct a spreadsheet based on the forecasts in Table 4.4 for a manufacturing company.

Use spreadsheet formulae to calculate:

◆ gross profit;

◆ net profit;

◆ gross profit margin;

◆ breakeven turnover;

◆ breakeven target per month.

Table 4.4   Profitable Manufacturing Company: twelve-month forecast

	£
Sales	200 000.00
Opening stock	70 000.00
Purchases	130 000.00
Closing stock	95 000.00
Materials costs	90 000.00
Wages	55 000.00
Fixed costs	30 000.00
Gross profit	= Profit before fixed costs
Net profit	= Profit after fixed costs
Profit margin	= Gross profit × 100 / Sales
Breakeven turnover	= Fixed costs × 100 / Profit margin
Breakeven target per month	= Breakeven turnover / 12

Assuming no seasonal (or other variations) in sales, and ignoring taxation, what is the forecast 12-month cash flow if average fixed costs (£) per month are:

1500	Premises rent, rates, heat and light, etc.
700	Loan repayments
300	Insurance and professional fees

Part Two

MANAGING INFORMATION

5 Information technology

Learning objectives

◆ To understand the main features of a computer.

◆ To outline the developmental stages in computer design and manufacture.

◆ To distinguish between different input and output devices, and identify each with its particular areas of application.

◆ To outline the main features and purpose of systems software.

◆ To identify the advantages of modern, fourth-generation programming languages over more conventional (third-generation) languages.

◆ To understand the basic structure of databases, distinguish between relational and hierarchical approaches, and list the advantages of the relational approach compared to more traditional file structures.

◆ To be aware of the importance of communication systems.

◆ To identify the main features and benefits of:
  – word processors;
  – spreadsheets;
  – desk-top publishing systems;
  – multimedia;
  – computer-aided design/computer-aided manufacture;
  – integrated office suites.

Computers

What is a computer?

Let us define it as:

> **A device which collects data, performs pre-programmed, high-speed arithmetic or logical operations upon it, and in doing so processes that data to produce either information, the automatic execution of some action, or both.**

With this definition in mind, consider the following familiar devices:

◆ video recorder;
◆ calculator;
◆ automatic washing machine;
◆ audio system;
◆ telephone answering machine;
◆ television receiver;
◆ personal computer;
◆ central heating controller;
◆ motor vehicle.

Nowadays, most of these possess some kind of *microprocessor* – something we associate with a computer. A video-cassette recorder, for example, inputs a program from its handset and then uses this data to perform (automatically) the actions necessary to record a television programme from a specified channel at some specified date and time. Washing machines, audio systems, televisions, cars, central heating systems and even some calculators are also programmable. Usually, they require a human operator to select from a finite set of programs. Only in the case of the personal computer is there infinite programmability, i.e. there are only practical limitations to the number and variety of programs or sets of instructions that can be executed. Indeed, given the appropriate connections, such a device could (and, if Bill Gates of Microsoft has his way, soon will) control all of these other devices – although cars, one hopes, will, at least for some time, retain a manual steering wheel and brakes in case of programmer error.

Of course, only the personal computer (frequently referred to, simply, as a *PC*) is actually referred to as a computer. This is for good reason. In practice, a computer is usually a general-purpose device, even though it may be dedicated in many cases to a limited set of tasks.

The development of computers

The modern computer – be it a PC or a large *mainframe* machine – is a fusion of certain developments in mathematics and logic with the modern science of electronics. Some of the most significant of these developments are discussed below.

Binary arithmetic (von Leibnitz, 1660)

The ability to represent any number (and, via a system of coding or mapping, any character or image) with a sequence of 0s and 1s associates perfectly with the on–off states of electrical and electronic systems. For example:

Decimal number 65 = 1000001 (binary) = 'A' (in *ASCII* – computer code)

Symbolic logic (Boole, 1854)

Boolean logic (or Boolean algebra) allows logical as well as arithmetic processes to be performed. This time, the on–off electronic state is represented, not as 0 or 1, but as true or false. The rules of Boolean algebra can be applied in the solution of any problem that has a true/false answer, and can consequently be used to form the basis of electronic circuits.

In the circuit shown in Fig. 5.1, for example, the Boolean expression would be:

$x = (i$ or $j)$ and k

x is true (on) if either i is true (on) OR j is true (on) AND k is true (on)

That is, if k is true and both i or j are false then x is also false.
If k is false then x is also false regardless of the state of i or j.

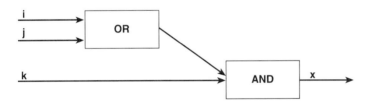

Fig 5.1   Logic circuit

Principles of universal computing (Turing, 1936, 1945)

Turing actually built a computer that was used to break German secret codes during the Second World War. His main contribution, however, is in providing a mathematical and theoretical basis for modern computing by conceiving a theory of automation (1936). His 'universal computer' could (at least on paper) solve virtually any mathematical or logical problem.

Stored program (von Neumann, 1947)

Von Neumann's computer design (or architecture) is still used today. Its basis is the presence of a serial processor, i.e. one which executes one instruction or operation at a time according to a pre-set sequence or program.

First stored-program computer (EDSAC, 1949)

This machine was developed at Cambridge some months before von Neumann's rival *EDVAC* design.

360 series computer (IBM, 1960s)

This was the first commercial machine to use integrated circuits. These avoided the mass of wires and soldered components of earlier designs, and were consequently faster and more reliable. The 360 sold in considerable numbers and provided the first general-purpose system. It revolutionised computing and ushered in the era of large (mainframe) computer systems, generally housed in vast, air-conditioned rooms and consisting of banks of floor-standing cabinets, housing processors, tape drives, discs, printers, etc. (*see* Fig. 5.2).

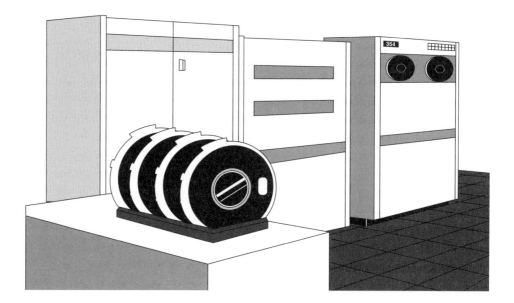

Fig 5.2   Mainframe computer

4004 microprocessor (Intel, 1971)

This was the first complete processor manufactured as a single slice (or chip) of silicon. It is this miniaturisation of electronic circuits which produced the revolution, since they now consumed far less power and produced very little heat. Furthermore, they are vastly less expensive to manufacture, are more reliable and, since electricity flows are shortened, have a correspondingly greater speed.

Personal computer (IBM, 1981)

This machine was not a revolutionary design, but it set the personal computer (PC) standard (IBM design or architecture, Intel processor and Microsoft operating system – *MSDOS* then *Windows*), which has prevailed to the present day. Moreover, although not displacing mainframes or mid-sized (mini) computers, the PC has, through sheer numbers of users, become the major driving force behind the spread and development of computerised systems and associated technologies.

Computer generations

This is a useful way of characterising the historical development of the computer from the late 1940s to the present. Each transition from one generation to the next has resulted in greater speed and more power, greater reliability and lower costs. We are now moving into the fifth generation of machines, with the path of progress remaining the same, i.e. the future is always more speed, greater power, lower cost and smaller size. Overall, the cumulative effect is to reduce cost by a factor of ten per decade, while increasing power by a factor of 100.

Let us look in outline at these changes. If we cut corners a little and associate each generation with a particular decade, we arrive at Table 5.1.

Table 5.1 Computer generations

Decade	Generation	Technology	No. of transistors	Memory
1950s	1st	Valves	—	0.4 KB
1960s	2nd	Transistors	< 100	8 KB
1970s	3rd	Integrated circuits (introduction of silicon)	< 2000	64 KB
1980s	4th	Very large-scale integration	< 2 million	5 MB
1990s	5th	Ultra large-scale integration	> 2 million	32 MB+

Another, more recent, perspective is to see development as a series of four waves. The first of these belongs to the mainframe. The second wave is the minicomputer. The third is the era of the PC. The fourth (and here we enter the realms of conjecture) belongs to the network, the Internet and the so-called *network computer (NC)*, or its rival project the *NetPC* – both are slimmed down PCs, designed especially for networks and claimed to be cheaper to buy and to own than existing standards.

Computer hardware

How does a computer work? Do we need to know? The answer (for all but computer specialists) is that, just as a rudimentary knowledge of car mechanics helps us to drive a little more safely and more economically, so a similar outline understanding of computer technology should help us to use it a little more efficiently.

The processor

Sometimes referred to as the central processing unit (CPU), the computer's processor performs arithmetic and logical operations, and controls both the sequential execution of each instruction, together with the transfer of data between input and output systems. There is also room within modern processors for a small amount of very fast memory circuits (*cache*), where data about to be processed is held.

Memory

The main memory inside a computer is regarded as short term and dynamic as opposed to the longer-term storage devices such as disc or compact disc. Sizes vary, but 8, 16 or even 32 megabytes (1 megabyte = one million bytes or characters) is now commonplace in personal computers. Access is very fast and is either with *random access memory (RAM)* or *read-only memory (ROM)*. The latter takes only a small portion of total memory locations and is usually used to store system configuration data (processor and disc type, etc.). This needs protection from being overwritten or lost on switch-off. Transfer to and from RAM is fast because the same silicon technology is used as in the processor itself.

Fixed data storage

This has a much greater capacity than RAM. Even desk-top personal computers now commonly possess fixed disc (or hard disc) sizes of 1 or 2 gigabytes (1 gigabyte equals one thousand million bytes or characters). Storage is semi-permanent in that data can be retained until erased by the user. Typically, fixed discs are used to store operating systems, databases, application programs and current data. If space is available they may also contain historical data but this is normally archived, either to another disc or some other storage medium. Disc drive technology is electro-mechanical (i.e. it contains both solid-state electronics and moving parts). As is the case with audio and video tape, reading and recording is via magnetic heads.

Removable data storage

Floppy discs

These have a much smaller capacity than fixed discs – typically 1.44 MB (although new systems promise far greater capacity). They are used for input (often to install programs) and for the transfer of data files from fixed disc drives, either for back-up purposes or for transfer to another computer.

CD-ROM

Compact discs are read-only technology, although some new devices allow write operations, giving them the same versatility as floppy discs but with much greater speed and capacity. CDs allow the storage and retrieval at acceptable speeds of the large volumes of data required to hold video and sound information. In fact, a new industry has emerged to publish computer CDs as multimedia titles, covering everything from games to encyclopaedias. CD-ROM technology is very similar to that of audio CDs. The latter can in fact be played (normally) through most computer CD drives, provided the computer itself has attached speaker systems or earphones.

Magnetic tape

This was the earliest form of volume data storage. It is still used in reel-to-reel machines where volumes of data are very large, but has been replaced in the majority of systems by disc drives. In cassette or cartridge format, magnetic tape has a smaller capacity and is used mainly in back-up systems and also for large-volume software installations. The design of these is similar to that of video cassettes.

User interface devices

The most common are the *keyboard*, *mouse* and *screen* (or *monitor*).

Less common but increasingly prominent are :

◆ *tracker-ball/pad* – used in portable (notebook) computers;

◆ *joystick* – used for games;

◆ *touch-screen* – used, for example, in public enquiry and information systems;

◆ *light-pen* – used as an alternative to a mouse for some applications;

◆ *speakers* – for multimedia software such as games or training programs;

◆ *microphone* – for voice controlled systems.

Scanning devices

These convert text or graphical images directly into computer-readable format. The most common are:

◆ *optical character readers (OCR)* – most read text only, but some specialised systems can recognise handwriting;

◆ *image scanners* – these create digitised maps of pictures for computer storage and subsequent editing;

◆ *digitisers* – for mapping coordinates;

◆ *bar-code readers* – used extensively in retailing, where products are identified and costed by a line of variable bars printed on packaging;

◆ *optical mark readers (OMR)* – most familiarly used in some exams and, of course, in the National Lottery;

◆ *magnetic strip* – widely used in credit and other cards which have information stored magnetically – cards can then be 'swiped' for on-line transactions.

Printers and plotters

These vary in type, speed and size according to requirements. On mainframe systems output is often to pre-printed stationery, with volumes demanding large, floor-standing printers combined with high-capacity stacking and hopper facilities.

Plain paper and envelope printing is often carried out on smaller desk-top *laser* printers. Unlike older ribbon printers, these are non-impact and therefore quiet in operation. Laser printers have a technology similar to that of the photocopier. They are found in large computer installations, often attached to a network to make them more accessible, but are also used by small business and home computer users. Where volumes are very small, however, many of these opt for low-cost *ink-jet* printers, which spray special fast-drying ink, and can be used with all types and sizes of stationery. This is a much slower (and more expensive process) than laser printing but the technology does have the advantage of allowing colour printing at a reasonable cost.

Colour printing is possible on lasers and is of much higher quality than is the case with ink-jets. However, colour lasers are too expensive for all but the specialist business and professional user. Publishing companies in particular are among the main users of high-quality laser equipment, much of it being carried out under the control of a special print language (*Postscript*), which is built into the printer itself.

Plotters use computer-controlled pens to draw output of any colour. They vary in size from A4 to A0, with computer-aided design applications, in particular, employing them to produce high-quality precision drawings.

Video and audio

One of the main reasons that computers have become more interesting to more people is their visual appeal. Most users find that a Microsoft Windows (or Apple) screen is easy to interact with and provides a more natural 'look and feel' than older, text-based designs. It is as if the computer has been made to work more in the way human beings do – which of course is what has happened.

If we feel more comfortable with a graphical screen, working with pictures as well as text, then we will undoubtedly feel even better (and work even more naturally) if we could listen and talk to the computer, and if we were able to view moving as well as still images.

With the single exception of voice recognition (i.e. using speech to operate the computer), which is still largely experimental and specialised in use, all of these technologies are well developed, or even commonplace. In fact, the expansion of audio and video linkage has been driven by the consumer rather than the corporate marketplace.

The main applications so far established (or at least envisaged) are:

◆ *multimedia* – this has become an umbrella term to refer to any computer application which communicates through sound, graphical images and video;

◆ *video conferencing* – an extension of computer networking and electronic mail which allows 'face-to-face' communication;

◆ *video-on-demand* – the transmission of digitised video via cable, terrestrial or satellite links;

◆ *computer animation* – the ease with which stored, digitised images can be manipulated has led to the development of new and much more powerful special effects techniques with seemingly limitless possibilities (cf. films such as *Jurassic Park*, *Mask*, or *Independence Day*).

To send and receive multimedia information, computers need to have the most powerful processors, large amounts of RAM, large fixed discs and CD-ROM. They also require fast audio and video circuits to compress and decode the data. Multimedia machines are therefore relatively expensive and, because of the importance of the home market, it is now common for many business desk-top machines to be less powerful and costly than their counterparts in the home.

Computer software

The industry which supplies computer software is vastly more significant and pervasive than that which provides the hardware. The latter is confined to a comparatively small number of manufacturers. The former includes a vast product range, from an individual manager's untutored efforts at report writing (using some 'user-friendly' programming language such as BASIC), to a giant corporation, such as Microsoft, which publishes everything from operating systems to electronic encyclopaedias.

Although boundaries are becoming somewhat blurred, it is still useful to categorise software as:

◆ systems software;
◆ programming languages;
◆ database management systems;
◆ network and communications management systems;
◆ application programs (or packages).

Systems software

This comprises *operating systems* and related utilities. Examples include:

MSDOS	(PCs)
Windows 3.x and 95	(PCs)
Windows NT	(PCs and mini-computers)
Apple	(PCs)
Novell	(PC networks)
UNIX	(minicomputers – non-proprietary)
AS400	(minicomputers – IBM)
VME	(mainframe – ICL)
MVS	(mainframe – IBM)

One of the most important kinds of system software to emerge in recent years is that concerned with access to the Internet and with enabling users to browse through the vast amount of information stored on the World-wide Web. More on this later.

Operating systems control and support computer operations and resources. They require at least the inclusion of:

◆ *a command processor* – executes commands input by the user (e.g. copy/delete/list/start a program);

◆ *a memory manager* – ensures sufficient memory is available and uniquely allocated to a particular program;

◆ *an input–output system* – controls the transfer of data to and from the central processor, memory and external devices;

◆ *a file management system* – controls the format, organisation and storage of files and (in multi-user systems) will also manage user access;

◆ *utilities* – a collection of programs which 'get the job done' (e.g. back-up systems, virus detection, resource accounting and diagnostic routines).

Programming languages

A common way of categorising these is to distinguish between low-level and high-level languages. Low-level language is (or is at least close to) what the computer actually understands. At the lowest level is the actual *machine language* (or code) which is composed entirely of 0s and 1s. High-level languages, on the other hand, are closer to human language. Indeed the quest is on for *natural language understanding* by the computer so that we can communicate with it as we do other human beings.

Another way is to use the same generation idea as we did when tracing the development of computers. So, we have the following.

First generation

This is actual machine code, so no translator is necessary. To use it, however, we must be content with expressing everything as sequences of 0s and 1s. This is difficult to say the least, and is extremely error-prone.

Second generation

These are translators (or assemblers) which employ a kind of shorthand (using mnemonics such as MOV (move) or STO (store) together with specified memory locations) to represent actual machine code.

Third generation

These are the high-level languages, the first of which (FORTRAN) dates from the mid-1950s. Other examples include, COBOL, C, Pascal and BASIC. Third generation languages (3GLs) are less machine-oriented, allowing subsets of English to be used. Programs consequently become much easier to write and read, and therefore to maintain. (Even non-experts, for example, can get some idea of what the program listings reproduced in Chapter 6 are actually about.) The other major advantage of high-level languages is that they are portable across different makes of computer, whereas machine or assembly languages are specific to, say, Intel processors and cannot be used on any other. Their one significant disadvantage is their need for translation into machine language. This process reduces processing speed below that which an experienced low-level programmer could achieve.

Fourth generation

First, second and third generation languages all have one thing in common – they are procedural. This means that the program starts at a particular point, follows a process or path to the end, and then finishes. This may not be how human beings actually work. It may be more appropriate for a program to be built as a series of events, any of which can be selected, individually, without reference to any other. Such non-procedural approaches offer more dialogue and choices for the user, and are also (potentially) easier to write, since they usually include powerful routines for automating the more common tasks – often without the need to write any code at all. Fourth generation languages (4GLs) offer a wide variety of formats and approaches. Some (e.g. Visual BASIC or Visual C) are really 3GLs with powerful enhancements which automate much of the chore of writing code, especially the creation of screen layouts and reports, both of which can be extremely time-consuming to write in a 3GL alone. Others, such as Structured Query Language (SQL), are aimed at non-programmers who wish to write their own database queries and reports without asking an expert to write a program for them. In practice, SQL has not proved that easy to use, and, although still widely used in its 'raw' state, it is now linked to graphical query systems. Using these, complex queries and reports can be generated, with a few mouse presses, by a dialogue which generates the appropriate SQL commands needed to extract the data.

Fifth generation

Almost all programs are now written with enhanced 3GLs or 4GLs. There is, as yet, no commercial example of a fifth generation language. This has not stopped developers envisaging what a 5GL would be like. In reality, it would be unlike anything that has gone before in both removing the need for expert programmers and in providing a natural language interface to the user.

One line of development towards this perfect state is the idea of using a high-level (or natural) language as a computer's machine language. If this were achieved, the computer would seem to have acquired intelligence, since language understanding is in itself an intelligent act. In their 'Fifth Generation Project', the Japanese looked at the feasibility of using the language Prolog in such a way. Prolog was designed to assist with developments in *artificial intelligence*, and although another language (LISP) dominates in the specialised field of robotics, Prolog has a much wider potential and is particularly suitable as a basis for natural language systems. This is partly because it is completely non-procedural – placing the emphasis on what is to be accomplished as opposed to how.

This difference may be explained through an analogy. Say we ask a friend for a lift to Sainsbury's. If he doesn't know the way, we could say that this is equivalent to a 3GL, i.e. we would need to specify in detail, and in correct sequence, all the steps necessary to get to our destination. We might say:

- *start;*
- *go straight for a mile;*
- *turn right;*
- *go straight for two miles;*
- *second left at roundabout;*
- *straight on for 300 yards;*
- *turn right;*
- *stop.*

If he knows part of the route we could say this was like a 4GL:

- *second left at the Cheadle Royal Roundabout;*
- *straight on for 300 yards;*
- *turn right;*
- *stop.*

If he knows all of the route, or can work it out from knowledge, then (as in a possible future 5GL) we would simply say:

- *take me to Sainsbury's.*

Database management systems

Examples are:

Oracle

Sybase

DB2

Access

Paradox

dBASE

Traditional data and file structures

Most kinds of information lend themselves to a format or structure which we commonly refer to as a data record. These are groupings of related data items, e.g. names and addresses. In older systems, data records are themselves grouped together in files so that a file containing name and address records would be separate from any other file and would hold only those records. (We will discuss data structures in more detail in the next chapter.)

The structure of such files is associated with the way in which access to a record is required. Access may be:

◆ *serial* – records are accessed in the physical order in which they reside within the file;

◆ *sequential* – records are accessed in logical order (e.g. alphabetically);

◆ *random* – individual records are accessed at random;

◆ *indexed-sequential* – both random and sequential access are possible.

The effects of these different types of access are demonstrated in Table 5.2.

Table 5.2   Types of file access

Physical order	Logical order	Serial access	Sequential access	Random access
Jones	Adams	Jones	Adams	Clark
Smith	Brown	Smith	Brown	
Brown	Clark	Brown	Clark	
Clark	Jones	Clark	Jones	
Adams	Smith	Adams	Smith	

Although *serial* access may be appropriate where very large volumes of data are to be read for summarisation (e.g. totalling or averaging), or where the storage medium is magnetic tape, the disadvantage of having to read every record to get at the ones selected will be familiar to anyone who has played the same music album on both tape and CD. *Sequential* access needs either an index to find selected records or these must first be sorted into their required logical order. Again, if magnetic tape is still employed, much processing time will be taken up with the prerequisite sorting operations. *Random* and *indexed-sequential* access can only be achieved with disc-based storage which has predefined tracks and movable read/write heads to allow direct access. Again the analogy is with CDs.

Database structures

The advantages of adopting database structures are so clear these have been replacing more traditional, file-based approaches for some years. One prerequisite is that all of an organisation's data needs to be described precisely and analysed for:

◆ *logical relationships* – e.g. names and addresses are related items;
◆ *duplication/redundancy* – e.g. if addresses are found in orders data, do they need also to be included with invoice data?

This needs to be done before rather than as programs are written. Programs are therefore designed to manipulate the data as it is already defined, rather than needing to create and manipulate their own data structures, which may be duplications or variations of others elsewhere. This separation of programs and data leads to simpler programs, shorter development times and more accurate processing.

Database management systems (DBMS)

These have elements which resemble operating systems. For example, they control the way data is stored, organised and accessed. Most also include their own (or use standard) programming and data-querying languages. These can be used to interrogate the underlying database and can also be employed to create complete, computerised applications.

All current developments in DBMS software aim to make programming redundant by replacing it with an interface to the data which is as close to natural language as is possible.

Although other approaches are still in use (some airline reservation systems, for example, use a *hierarchical* database structure which can also be structured to mirror the organisation as in Fig. 5.3), most DBMS now employ a *relational* approach. This means that all the data is held as simple tables from which the relationships between data items can be created.

Relational database tables (*see* Fig. 5.4) consist of rows and columns. Each row defines a data record. Columns represent individual data items. Tables can be linked (or joined) together via relationships created between one or more of their data items. These table *joins* can then be used to create new permanent tables, or to build less permanent data *views*. These can then form the basis for database queries.

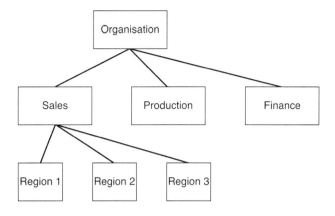

Fig 5.3   Hierarchical database structure

Since these data views are based on tables which are dynamically linked, any change to particular records will be reflected in related data. In a sales table, for example, any change to unit price would trigger a change in a related table containing sales revenues. There is no risk to the accuracy or status of any record through duplication or simultaneous updates by different users, since all data has *integrity*, i.e. there is only one current version. Their comparative simplicity, together with this ease of relation and corresponding data integrity, constitute the major advantages of relational systems.

Last Name	First Name	Job	DOB	Hire Date	Address
Taylor	Nancy	Sales Assistant	01-Dec-45	2-Mar-89	21 East Street
Miller	Peter	Sales Assistant	29-Apr-44	11-Jun-94	301 West Way
Lever	Jane	Sales Manager	3-Sep-63	20-Feb-89	102 South Road
Peabody	Barbara	Receptionist	9-Mar-73	31-Aug-91	40 North Road
Butcher	Frank	Sales Representative	14-Jul-59	1-Oct-91	21 East End

Fig 5.4   Relational database table

Some of the advantages of linking may be seen in Fig. 5.5. Links between the three tables prevent the need to duplicate the data element *department_name*, in every staff details record. They would also allow salary cost analysis to be carried out without the overhead of staff detail, such as name and address data. Following linkage, the resultant data view can be used for queries or reports, and retained or discarded as required. Another important advantage is that relationships between data items are not fixed but can be revised by system administrators as managers find new ways of analysing the data.

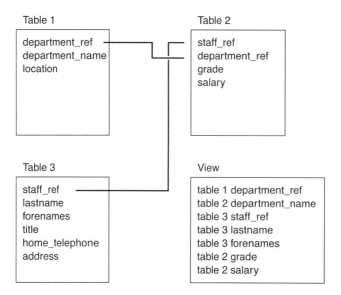

Fig 5.5   Table linkage and related table view

It is important to note that these data relations operations and table management are largely hidden from the user, as are the routines necessary to maintain the accuracy, integrity and security of the data. Non-expert users are able to manipulate and extract data without reference to this underlying process. Furthermore, the use of analytical aids, such as graphical query builders, executive information systems and decision support systems (*see* Chapter 6 for more on these), makes the task even more straightforward.

In another development, even modern relational systems are beginning to face competition from alternative *object-oriented* technologies – again, more in the next chapter.

Communication Systems

Why is communication between computers so important? Computer networking has in fact become so prominent in both business and popular culture that the future is often seen as a world dominated by our ability to have instant access to anyone, or anywhere, in the world – and beyond?

The transmission of information between computers requires:

◆ a transmitter/receiver (modem or ISDN connection);

◆ a channel (cable, or microwave frequency);

◆ communication software and protocol;

◆ a suitable operating system (i.e. one which can incorporate the connection or network).

Modems convert the digital signal of the computer into an *analogue* form (i.e. continuous as opposed to a binary on off signal) suitable for transmission along a telephone line. ISDN connections do the same job, but are much faster because the digital to analogue conversion is unnecessary. Communications software may consist of simple, inexpensive (sometimes free) programs, which manage electronic mail and the transfer of files between computers that may be locally or remotely connected. Protocols define the agreed standards for getting computers to 'talk' to one another. For example, the standard protocol for the Internet is called TCP/IP.

Other examples are much more complex and expensive. These (e.g. UNIX, Novell Netware and Microsoft NT) are full-blown operating systems that control the sharing of application software as well as the exchange of information between users. Again these facilities may be on a single site or cover a wide area.

Local area networks (LAN)

If there is a requirement to connect a number of computers together on a single site, a simple local area network can be created using cheap coaxial cable and connectors (similar to television aerial wiring). Transmission speed is low but adequate unless a large number of users are sharing applications or using multimedia files. In these cases, optical fibre cable, which has greater speed and *bandwidth* (i.e. number of possible simultaneous transmissions), is necessary, although more expensive. It is also usual to install a central powerful computer (or *server*) to hold common databases, documents, applications, etc.

Wide area networks (WAN)

If the need to network extends beyond a single site, organisations must use either their own dedicated transmission lines or pay for the use of public channels. These may be cable or microwave (or a combination of both), using technology similar to that of telephone or mobile (cellular) connections. Satellites can also be used to provide channels, using technology similar to that of satellite television broadcasting. A major trend in all of these areas, as in terrestrial television broadcasts, is to move from analogue to digital transmission.

The Internet

The Internet is based on an agreed set of rules *(protocols)* which make possible the connection of any computer to any other computer throughout the world, provided it is connected to a communications channel.

At first the preserve of academics and computer hobbyists, the Internet is now becoming as established for general use as is the international telephone network, upon which of course it depends. Along with this increased profile and popularity has come new terminology (cf. the *information superhighway*) and an extension of the original electronic mail and file transfer facilities to full multimedia communication. The resultant *World-wide Web (WWW)* is a global collection of sites (i.e. reserved space on host computers) where all kinds of information is stored and made accessible in so-called *home pages*. It is to these (and to national, international, academic and business databases) that 'web-' or 'net-surfers' travel to via 'cyber-space'.

The Internet is undoubtedly here to stay and will grow and develop. There is even a spin-off technology, the *Intranet*, which has local area networks being run to the same protocols and by similar software. With this approach, users may be unaware if they are browsing a local or a remote database.

Browsing the Internet's computers is facilitated by the use of a special program which helps the user locate a site and then displays the information in a format which makes further searching easier through the use of active links to related sites. In the latest versions of these *browsers*, it is also possible to embed applications (e.g. a word processor), written in a special language called *Java*. When these developments are complete, it should be possible to conduct all computer operations (network or stand-alone) via this single browser screen.

There are, unfortunately, some problems to be overcome before the Internet fulfils its promise. The main questions are concerned with:

◆ *bandwidth* – if everyone joins and more data is multimedia, present channels will not cope;

◆ *security* – if business and financial transactions are to travel the Internet more attention will have to be given to protection from viruses and fraudsters;

◆ *cost* – subscription rates and telephone charges can be significant for all but occasional use;

◆ *quality* – finding what you want can involve trawling through oceans of mediocrity, the downright dreadful and even the pornographic before you arrive;

◆ *computer ownership* – contrary to some expectations, we are still far away from having a computer in every home. A move to television-connected, cheap Internet terminals might help, but take-up by the general public is by no means assured.

Application software

Examples include:

accounting and financial management;

banking and insurance;

computer-aided design and manufacture;

education, training and research;

government (Inland Revenue, Social Security, Treasury, etc.);

word processing and publishing;

personnel management and payroll;

policing;

production control, scheduling and route finding;

spreadsheet modelling;

stock control;

stock market and share management;

travel reservations.

In the early days of computing, applications were 'bespoke', i.e. they were written for a particular purpose and organisation, often by the organisation itself. The incorporation of local features and needs in their design was consequently natural. However, since programming in conventional 3GLs is highly skilled, time-consuming and error-prone, software costs were extremely high, and could only be afforded by large companies or government departments. Where software was not written 'in-house', a further cost was associated with the high dependency, which inevitably became established, between user and software supplier, who was often also the supplier of computer hardware. Once embarked upon a particular path with one of these (more often than not IBM), it was difficult and expensive for any organisation to extricate itself from this relationship. This situation reduced competition.

A great deal of software is still bespoke, although much of it nowadays is produced by specialised consulting companies which undertake everything from analysis to implementation. (Increasingly, these companies also take over the actual operation of computer systems and computer personnel in a process known as *facilities management* – more on this later.) Although 4GLs are now used, costs remain high, sometimes running to millions, even hundreds of millions of pounds.

Since the 1980s, and associated with the microcomputer revolution, the trend has been to move away from this approach as far as possible. Standard 'off-the-shelf' software packages have now opened the market and reduced costs dramatically. Initially embraced by smaller organisations, packages such as Lotus 1-2-3, WordPerfect, Word, Excel, Access, Foxpro and dBASE have also been taken up by larger users. The use of some programs (notably Excel, Word and WordPerfect) is now so universal (users run to several millions world-wide), they have almost become international standards in themselves.

In addition to reduced costs, the introduction of standard packages has resulted in software of a much higher quality and ease of use than hitherto. This is a consequence of the size of investment possible and the competitive marketplace. If your potential market is numbered in millions, you get your product right first time and try to keep it ahead of the field.

There are disadvantages. A package will rarely do things exactly in the way users require. If they are unwilling (or unable) to adapt procedures to fit, extensive changes to the package may be necessary and costly. Moreover, dependence has not been entirely eradicated. A company which moves its accounting systems on to a particular package, for example, could well be in some difficulty if its supplier went out of business or refused to continue support. In practice, although software publishers sometimes come and go with alarming rapidity, the more popular systems will always find at least sufficient support and continued development to allow an orderly transfer by the user to a rival system.

 # Features of application software

This book is obviously no place for instruction in the use of actual software packages. Here we will concentrate on the major features of some of the more popular applications, and also outline their major benefits to users.

Word processors

Examples include:

Microsoft Word;

Corel WordPerfect;

Lotus WordPro.

Although there is still a large reservoir of trained and professional typists, for most of us, the experience of having to produce something (even as short as a letter) on a typewriter is profoundly frustrating. Mistakes are inevitable, corrections are slow and imperfect, major rethinks involve a fresh start – and there is no one to help with our spelling. Modern word processors dismiss all of these difficulties, while also providing an array of facilities for the creation, editing, formatting and printing of both text and graphics to a quality, hitherto, only attainable by professional publishers.

The main features of a modern word processor include:

◆ *document management* – creation/save/filing;

◆ *templates* – pre-formatted for common types of document (e.g. letters, memos, reports, etc.);

◆ *page layout* – paper size, margins, footnotes, headers, line spacing, page numbering, etc.;

◆ *print preview* – view as printed;

◆ *edit* – full page – with copy, cut and paste, etc.;

◆ *find/replace* – global or individual text find and revision;

◆ *insert object* – allows insert at any point of other documents, graphics, spreadsheets, databases – even audio and video;

◆ *format* – wide range of styles, borders and shading, text alignment, columns and tables;

◆ *other* – spelling, thesaurus, mail-merge, on-line help, etc.

Packages such as Microsoft Word or WordPerfect have a vast installed base. Since organisations normally standardise on one system, a number of other advantages also ensue:

◆ Software costs are reduced with bulk purchase or site licence.

◆ Training time and costs are reduced.

◆ Document standards can easily be maintained.

◆ Where computers are linked, communication can be paperless, with electronic mail systems allowing the transmission of whole documents from one user to another. Reports can be distributed, discussed and revised before final publication.

◆ Since occasional/unskilled operation can produce good results, the pressure on skilled operators or typists is reduced.

In fact, practically the only real disadvantage associated with the use of word processors (apart from purchase cost) is over-indulgence. This is the tendency to produce documents that are either unnecessary or over-long, or are over-elaborate in style and layout for the purpose in hand.

Spreadsheets

Examples include:

Microsoft Excel;

Lotus 1-2-3;

Quattro.

The development of computerised spreadsheets is closely associated with the development of the personal computer. Although they were available at first on mainframes, they were little used until the arrival in 1979 of a PC program called VisiCalc.

Most people have used a paper spreadsheet at one time or another. A shopping list of items to buy with expected purchase prices is a simple example. Another familiar use is in bank statements, where income and expenditure are listed and totalled. They are a completely natural way of keeping track of items and related facts, by separating each item in its own row, with columns representing the related information. However, the disadvantages of manual spreadsheets are fairly obvious:

◆ Mistakes are easily made and are difficult to correct.

◆ When individual items are changed, totals must be recalculated.

◆ It is difficult to insert new items.

◆ Anything beyond a very simple layout quickly gets out of hand. We forget any associations we may have made, and calculation becomes ever more difficult.

◆ Any kind of analysis of the information is difficult and involves operations and calculations which are of necessity outside the spreadsheet itself.

The main features of a modern spreadsheet package are as follows.

File management

Like word processor documents, spreadsheets are saved as files. In most cases, multiple related sheets can be opened and saved as one file or workbook.

Edit

Cell contents can be edited, cut, copied, deleted or moved with a few simple mouse presses. Formulae entered into a cell can be quickly copied to apply to related rows or columns to rapidly build a large spreadsheet.

Insert

The contents of other spreadsheets, documents, graphical images and charts can be inserted anywhere in the sheet.

Graphing

Most forms of graph can be drawn automatically from spreadsheet data.

'What if?'

Spreadsheets are ideal for forecasting since adjustment in intermediate figures is automatically reflected in related totals. If an economist wishes to predict the varying consequences of a change in interest rates, it is comparatively easy to apply different rate possibilities to a spreadsheet model and then see the different outcomes. The model must first be set up with appropriate formulae and figures relating to the area under analysis (e.g. industrial production totals per month by industry), but once this has been done, it may be used again and again to forecast different outcomes.

In a variation on the 'what if' scenario, most systems possess a feature which prompts the user for a target cell in which it will store optimal solutions to particular problems. For example, a sales manager might allocate a cell as 'maximised profit (%)', and ask the computer to adjust figures (regional or salesperson targets, say), within specified constraints, until the target figure is indeed maximised. In other words (in a reversal of 'what if' – which uses input to produce possible goals), we start with the goal and the computer delivers the necessary input.

Macros

A spreadsheet macro is a set of instructions or operations which might have been entered one by one, but which instead are executed automatically whenever the macro is run. In this sense, it is similar to a program – the major difference being that macros are usually limited in scope (and therefore in size), and are also, frequently, no more than recorded sets of keyboard or mouse presses. The user sets the spreadsheet on record and then performs the chosen sequence, which is saved and named as a macro. This is an enormous time-saver, even in the case of small macros. In many instances, however, sets of related macros are strung together in what becomes a completely automated process. In this way, spreadsheets can be used to develop end-user applications, especially if extra routines are available to quickly generate menus, data-entry screens and reports, etc.

Database

Most spreadsheets can operate as databases, allowing data to be sorted, filtered, totalled and grouped. It is also possible to connect to external databases, from which data can be extracted directly into the spreadsheet.

Spreadsheet packages are second in importance only to the word processor in the market for general purpose software packages. Although, in design, they seem to concentrate on statistics, accounting and financial management, their range of use is virtually limitless. In its time the most successful package, Lotus 1-2-3, was so named because it claimed to incorporate word processing and database facilities in addition to its spreadsheet, and this is now true of all systems. With the advent of graphical interfaces and high-resolution printers, all also possess integrated presentation graphics which are normally adequate for all but the most demanding presentation. Especially useful is the integration of data with graphs. This means that graphs are automatically redrawn whenever change occurs in the underlying spreadsheet.

Much of the development now taking place in spreadsheet technology surrounds their connectivity with other systems, especially with databases and word processors. One increasingly common arrangement is to have a mainframe or minicomputer (housing a large, corporate database and bespoke applications), with networked PCs used as 'intelligent' terminals. Unlike the dumb terminals (or VDUs) of the traditional mainframe set-up, PCs have their own processing power and application software. It therefore becomes a simple matter to interface this with the main database so that users can view data in their favourite spreadsheet format. This is especially useful for managers, who will normally not have the time to become specialist operators of the main system.

Desk-top publishing (DTP)

Examples include:

> *Adobe Pagemaker;*
>
> *Corel Ventura;*
>
> *Quark Xpress.*

Desk-top publishing is the extension of word processing to include graphics, artwork and photographic images, as well as text. Modern word processors also include these features, but, in a full DTP package, they are more powerful and more fully developed. In particular, the ability to use multi-columns, flow text around pictures, scan photographs and run at very high image resolutions is very much the province of professional DTP.

A typical DTP set-up would include:

◆ *a powerful desk-top computer* – Apple machines still dominate in the smaller installations, but in others, PCs and powerful UNIX systems are used. Larger installations, especially newspaper publishers, would normally link these in a network with a minicomputer at its centre;

◆ *desk-top publishing software* – this would probably be combined with specialised artwork, drawing and photo-finish programs such as Corel Draw;

◆ *a high-resolution laser printer* – at least a resolution of 600 × 600 dots per inch;

◆ *image scanning equipment* – usually a flat-bed device for photographs etc.;

◆ *high-resolution monitor* – this would be of comparatively large size to aid composition (at least 20 inch) but may alternatively be of A4 proportions.

Lower-cost DTP equipment has revolutionised the world of professional publishing. Books, magazines, newspapers, advertising literature, newsletters, etc., can all be produced more quickly and at vastly reduced cost than hitherto. It is now possible, for example, to introduce a new national newspaper to the market so quickly and inexpensively that circulation figures do not have to be very large to cover costs. Not surprisingly, however, competition and lowered prices are forcing this margin ever downwards.

Multimedia software

Unfortunately, in the world of computing, 'buzzwords' and hype are particularly rife. If today's buzzwords are *information superhighway* and *net-surfing*, then undoubtedly yesterday's was *multimedia*. This does not mean, of course, that the concept has failed, merely that it is now taken for granted.

Incorporating sound and video with graphics and text, these systems are particularly associated with CD-ROM, powerful desk-top computers and a new software market, *edutainment*. The kind of hardware set-up ideal for games-playing also happens to be ideal for education and training packages, both of which require interaction between user and machine in a manner never before possible.

Multimedia is a marriage between DTP, word processing software and games technology. However, systems which have been developed specifically for the production of educational and training material usually involve the use of what are called *authoring systems*. These automate the integration of text, sound, graphics and video in such a way that material is presented interactively. Using such systems, it is theoretically possible for teachers to quickly create comprehensive and attractive learning packages. In practice, although small publications are often made in this way, larger, professional learning (or *computer-based training* – *CBT*) packages, are usually written by dedicated and trained staff. CBT packages are increasingly used by large organisations to cover at least part of their training programmes, with the *interactive video* features in particular being seen to be of great benefit to the training process. For schools and colleges there is a growing industry, much of it allied to the major book publishers, which provides similar material, although here cost is an important constraint.

Computer-aided design/computer-aided manufacture (CAD/CAM)

CAD is a specialised, high-resolution and high-precision drawing application which enables 3D representation of any drawing and allows rotation around any axis. These systems assist architects, engineers, fashion and other designers to draft their designs very much more quickly and cheaply than is possible manually. It is also possible, in some fields of application, to automatically translate a computer-produced drawing into actual reality via an integrated CAM process. The design of a motor vehicle construction, for example, may be automated right from its original conception to the actual fabrication process carried out with a computer-controlled steel press. The creativity is still human but the productivity gains are enormous. The risk factor in any new design is also reduced to the extent that engineering problems can be simulated and consequently foreseen.

Integrated office suites

Right from the early days of standard software package production, it was realised that the majority of computer users needed only a word processor, a spreadsheet, some form of presentation software and (possibly) a database. Although individual programs continued to concentrate on one or the other of these, most publishers produced, in addition, some form of integrated system which included all of these elements. Some early examples, e.g. Lotus Symphony, together with some dedicated mainframe packages (from IBM and ICL, etc.), tried to cover all aspects thoroughly, and therefore ended up being highly complex (and expensive) and were difficult to use. Over the last few years, truly integrated packages have continued to be available (e.g. Microsoft Works, Claris Works), but these have tended to become inexpensive, relatively lightweight, easy-to-use starter systems aimed at small businesses and the home user. The more heavyweight examples are being gradually replaced by what are called 'suites'. These are separate programs (word processor, spreadsheet, presentation graphics, database) but they are marketed as one system – and at a much lower price than if the individual items were bought separately. Overwhelmingly, the market leader is Microsoft Office, but there are also rival products from Lotus and Corel. The claim in each case is that, although each program is independent, the ease with which it can be integrated with other parts of the suite is such that data transfer from one to another is virtually seamless. Since these systems all operate from within a Windows environment and observe some standard data transfer protocol, this is largely true. However, any inexperienced user faced with the task of conducting a mail-merge in Microsoft Office as opposed to Microsoft Works might disagree.

Summary

- We began by defining the computer as a programmable, general-purpose, electronic machine for the processing of information. Its development has been a fusion of mathematics, logic and electronics in a process often characterised as a progression of computer generations.

- The major internal components and common external devices are associated with the need to:

  – carry out arithmetic and logical operations;

  – store small volumes of data (dynamically) for rapid access;

  – store larger volumes of data permanently if necessary – either on fixed or removable media;

  – collect data in machine-readable form;

  – output data and information in a format appropriate for a particular use.

- Software can be categorised as:

  – systems software;

  – programming languages;

  – database management systems;

  – network and communications management;

  – applications.

- Operating systems constitute the major portion of *systems software* and are basic to the underlying control and operation of the computer. The different generations of *programming languages* reflect the underlying changes in computer technology. In particular, modern fourth (and even fifth) generation languages are closer to natural language, but require much more powerful hardware to run upon.

- *Database* systems and structures have increasingly replaced more traditional file structures and related programs. The advantages are realised in ease of use and flexibility, but there are also benefits to application development which is now possible without programming.

- *Communication* between computers, either locally or via long-distance (even global) networks such as the Internet, is now of overwhelming importance, and is seen by many to constitute the future of computing. Also of great and increasing significance, standard *application packages* have in many areas replaced earlier bespoke systems.

- The major software packages will in the future influence virtually everyone in their workplace. Word processors are most common, but increasing use is also being made of spreadsheets, graphics and multimedia applications, while there is a widening relevance of the more specialised software which automates publishing and design, and many manufacturing processes.

Assignments

1 Describe in non-technical terms what a future ('millennium') computer might be like, and what features it might provide its user.

2 Since it is possible to have a computer built exactly to your specification, what would you specify for your own personal use? Consider reasonable cost constraints and include requirements for:

◆ processor and memory;

◆ storage;

◆ monitor;

◆ input and output devices.

3 Describe your route to college (or any other destination) as it might be expressed in a third generation language.

4 If you have access to a networked computer, learn how to create, send and access on-line, electronic mail.

Case study – the Internet

This study is an attempt to give the reader a short guide to the Internet, and to encourage activities which involve gaining access to it. If access is available, the list of sites and suggested searches given below is intended as a resource to assist first attempts at undertaking research via the Internet. It will become clear during this process that the two greatest difficulties facing the researcher are slow access speeds and the poor quality of much of the material. However, things are improving. There are some excellent pages, especially those belonging to national news and media groups, and the large corporations. There are also some useful so-called 'search engines' to help if you want to go further afield.

What is it?

The Internet is a network of networks. It connects millions of computers around the world, including the one you use when you access it. It is a vast source of information and is constantly changing and expanding.

It started life in the United States in the 1960s as part of the American reaction to Soviet space technology successes. Grants were made available, new computers were acquired and (most significantly) the idea grew that these systems should be linked so that scientists and academics could communicate their ideas and research to one another.

What was new about these networks (and what underlies the whole nature of the Internet which grew out of them) was the idea of *packet switching*. Packets of information are sent from one computer to another without the exact route specified in advance. The origin and destination is known, but it can have any number of forwarding addresses along the way. Because of this, packets intermingle with all the others in transit. There is no central station or hub. Consequently, if one computer goes down, another takes over. The network is 'self-healing' and, to some extent, self-regulating.

What does it provide?

E-mail

Because the user accesses the Internet at the nearest location, the telephone call-time costs are almost always at local rates. This means that, providing two individuals each have e-mail addresses, they can send and receive any type of information, from a simple text message to sound and video, inexpensively and conveniently. It also means that they can widen their discussions to include other parties, creating forums, news groups and conferences on-line.

File transfer

This includes application programs, graphic images, video and sound, as well as documents. This means that all kinds of software can be distributed over the network, including commercial film and music productions.

Remote log-in

Normal Internet use involves downloading information and files from another computer. What if we could actually operate that computer from our own desktop? Subject, of course to security measures, this facility creates tremendous power potential for the humble desk-top system.

World-wide Web

This is *the* Internet application. When the majority of people think of the Internet, they think of the Web. It is based on *hypertext* links and interactive multimedia. In a typical Web page (or site), underlined or emboldened text provides the links to other pages or sites. When one of these is selected, the linked page is accessed. This will usually contain further links, and so on. The user can easily backtrack to his starting location if required, and this, conveniently, will indicate the routes already taken. Where a site has embedded multimedia (video and sound clips, animation and images) this can be activated in the same way and, providing the computer being used for access has sound and video capabilities, we can see and hear as we might with a television or audio system.

Browsing the Web

Most readers of this book will have access to collegiate or public Internet services. If you have to arrange your own Internet access you will need :

◆ *a PC with modem and telephone point*;

◆ *an Internet service provider (ISP)* – you do not need to look for these – they will find you. ISP provide the software and getting-connected know-how. Some are large, on-line information services (such as CompuServe, AOL or MSN); others are smaller, specialist providers, located up and down the country;

◆ *somewhere to start* – your ISP will provide this, but some popular sites are listed in Tables 5.3 and 5.4.

Shopping on the Web – Barclaysquare

What happens if you combine the nation's two most popular pastimes: watching TV and shopping? You have a killer application. Substitute a computer for the TV and you have credit-card wonderland.

Many readers of this book will remember an advertisement for Fiat which depicted two teenagers, an interactive video of two dancing cars and an understanding father. All the major car manufacturers do in fact use the Internet for marketing their products. But what if, instead of one product, we could browse an entire shopping centre and buy anything we wanted via the desk-top?

Barclaysquare (http://www.itl.net/barclaysquare) is a virtual shopping mall backed by Barclays Bank. As the following description shows, this is a serious and pioneering business venture.

Barclaysquare – Banking on Net Surfers

Boasting up to 14 virtual 'shops', including BT, Toys R Us, J Sainsbury and Argos, Barclaysquare is a vision of what shopping will be like in the future. No more trudging through packed super-market aisles filled with screaming kids – instead, people will be able to go shopping via their PC screens, pay for goods at the click of a button, and wait for them to be delivered to their homes. According to one UK-based report, up to 2% of consumer shopping will be done electronically by the end of the decade.

Tony Slater, director of sales and marketing at Barclays Merchant, says: 'The Internet offers enormous benefits to small businesses by giving them the opportunity to compete with some of the high street's biggest names in a cost-effective way. With the Internet, small businesses can keep their doors open 24 hours a day without having to find new premises or employ additional staff.'

Barclaysquare lets customers browse through the online offerings of its stores before choosing an item and going to a virtual check out. There, customers are requested to enter credit card details. These are then encrypted using a combination of Netscape security software and security enhancements from ITL and Barclays Merchant Services.

Source: Computing, 28 March 1996.

Table 5.3   Alphabetical listing of popular Web sites

Site	Address	Category
100 Hot Sites	http://www.100hot.com	Search facility or directory
Alta Vista	http://www.altavista.digital.com	Search facility or directory
Apple	http://www.apple.com	Computing
BBC TV	http://www.bbc.org	Media
British Telecom	http://www.bt.com	Telecommunications
CBS Network	http://www.cbs.com	Media
CNN	http://www.cnn.com	News service
CNN Financial News	http://www.cnnfn.com	News service
Company directory	kttp://www.companies.whowhere.com	Search facility or directory
Cyberzine	http://www.cyberzine.com	Media
Discovery TV Channel	http://www.discovery.com	Media
Emap directory	http://www.emap.com/id/uk	Search facility or directory
European sites	http://www.euro.net	Search facility or directory
Excite	http://www.excite.com	Search facility or directory
Financial Times	http://www.ft.com	News service
Guardian	http://www.guardian.co.uk	News service
IBM	http://www.ibm.com	Computing
Intel	http://www.intel.com	Computing
Lycos	http://www.lycos.com	Search facility or directory
MacMillan Publishers	http://www.mcp.com	Media
Microsoft	http://www.microsoft.com	Computing
Muscat	http://www.muscat.co.uk	Search facility or directory
NASA	http://www.nasa.gov	Government
Parliament	http://www.parliament.uk	Government
Pathfinder	http://www.pathfinder.com	Search facility or directory
Prestel City News	http://www.citiservice.co.uk	News service
Prime Minister's Office	http://www.number-10.gov.uk	Government
Sunday Times	http://www.sunday-times.co.uk	News service
Telegraph	http://www.telegraph.co.uk	News service
Times	http://www.times.co.uk	News service
UK Government	http://www.open.gov.uk	Government
UK Internet Directory	http://www.ukindex.co.uk	Search facility or directory
Universal Studios	http://www.mca.com	Media
Warner Bros	http://www.warnerbros.com	Media
Webcrawler	http://www.webcrawler.com	Search facility or directory
White House	http://www.whitehouse.gov	Government
World Village	http://www.worldvillage.com	Search facility or directory
Yahoo sports index	http://www.sports.yahoo.com	Search facility or directory
Yahoo UK	http://www.yahoo.co.uk	Search facility or directory
Yellow Pages	http://www.yell.co.uk	Search facility or directory

Table 5.4 Popular Web sites by category

Site	Address
Computing	
Microsoft	http://www.microsoft.com
IBM	http://www.ibm.com
Apple	http://www.apple.com
Intel	http://www.intel.com
UK Government	http://www.open.gov.uk
Parliament	http://www.parliament.uk
Prime Minister's Office	http://www.number-10.gov.uk
White House	http://www.whitehouse.gov
NASA	http://www.nasa.gov
Media	
Warner Bros	http://www.warnerbros.com
CBS Network	http://www.cbs.com
MacMillan Publishers	http://www.mcp.com
Discovery TV Channel	http://www.discovery.com
Cyberzine	http://www.cyberzine.com
Universal Studios	http://www.mca.com
BBC TV	http://www.bbc.org
News services	
Financial Times	http://www.ft.com
Guardian	http://www.guardian.co.uk
Telegraph	http://www.telegraph.co.uk
Sunday Times	http://www.sunday-times.co.uk
Times	http://www.times.co.uk
Prestel City News	http://www.citiservice.co.uk
CNN	http://www.cnn.com
CNN Financial News	http://www.cnnfn.com
Search facilities	
Yahoo UK	http://www.yahoo.co.uk
Excite	http://www.excite.com
UK Internet Directory	http://www.ukindex.co.uk
Yahoo sports index	http://www.sports.yahoo.com
Pathfinder	http://www.pathfinder.com
Webcrawler	http://www.webcrawler.com
Lycos	http://www.lycos.com
Alta Vista	http://www.altavista.digital.com
100 Hot Sites	http://www.100hot.com
European sites	http://www.euro.net
World Village	http://www.worldvillage.com
Yellow Pages	http://www.yell.co.uk
Company directory	kttp://www.companies.whowhere.com
Muscat	http://www.muscat.co.uk

Your own Web site

And, finally. If you or your college or workplace subscribe to the Internet, why not have your own site on the World-wide Web? Most service providers allow space on their computers for users to upload their pages and consequently make them accessible all over the globe. All you need is a special editing programme which produces the special hypertext document format. The special formatting is referred to as hypertext mark-up language (*HTML*). As you read this, HTML editing should be available in all the mainstream word processors. If it is not, you will need a special editor, which you can download from the Internet. Some even include 'wizard' assistants which automate much of the process.

The important considerations in designing web pages are:

◆ *make it interesting* – if there are millions of pages, why should anyone stop at yours?

◆ *keep it uncluttered* – the viewer needs to find his way easily around the site, therefore make links logical and necessary, and provide a straightforward route back;

◆ *go easy on the graphics* – most people who may access your site will not have fast enough access speed to view complex graphics easily, and will therefore get frustrated and move on.

6 Information systems

Learning objectives

◆ To understand the concepts of information, system and management as components of a formal management information system.

◆ To recognise the importance of data within an organisation and identify the sources and flow of data both within the organisation and between it and its external environment.

◆ To evaluate the scope and purpose of a management information system.

◆ To outline the methods employed to ensure the proper design of a management information system and identify inherent weaknesses and consequent attempts at overcoming these.

◆ To describe the major components of a management information system as they impact the user and recognise some recent trends in developing interfaces between user and system.

Not all, but most, information systems involve technology. Not all, but most, information systems produce information for management. Our assumption here, therefore, is to make little or no distinction between the terms *computerised management information system (CMIS), management information system (MIS)* and *information system (IS)*.

In the previous chapter, we examined *information technology (IT)*, i.e. computer hardware and software, and communications equipment. We can now turn to the other components and examine them individually and together, to arrive at an overall understanding of the nature and features of management information systems, both as they exist today and what they may look like in the near future. We start with *information*.

 ## Information

Why do barriers develop around most fields of specialist activity? One reason is the tendency for experts to take ownership of particular words or phrases and to reduce their meaning to a greater precision than is generally the case in ordinary life. In general use, the terms *fact, data, information* and *knowledge* are often used interchangeably. A barrister, for example, would discuss the *facts* of a case with the defendant, examine *data* contained in relevant documents, use *information* provided by informants, who may, in the first place, have volunteered *facts* and *data* to the police. Finally, the barrister would use *knowledge* gained from the evidence, so acquired, in advocacy to the jury.

However, the specialists who develop management information systems use these terms much more distinctly. *Data* refers specifically to *facts* which have been organised in some way and is separated in meaning from the other three words. An individual's age, for instance, is a factual item which forms part of our description of that person. If he or she belongs to a certain group of people, we could obtain a data-set of all their ages:

Name	Age
Matthews, J.	92
Matthews, A.	78
Jones, H.	34
Jones, P.	45
Wiiliams, K.	89
Williams, M.	21
Halliwell, S.	91
Taylor, L.	78
Marsh, R.	14
Marsh, T.	77

Average age = 61.9

Unfortunately, unless the group is very small, this will not provide us with any information about the group, only of the individuals within it. So we summarise. We calculate the average age. This is *information* about the group. Their average age is 61.9 years. We could conclude, therefore, that they will retire soon and so provision must be made for pensions and healthcare, etc. But is this true? Certainly not for at least four of the individuals here. Because we have not yet applied intelligence, or any relevant experience, in our consideration of this information, we may not yet possess the *knowledge* upon which rests our best chance of making correct decisions with any degree of consistency. In this example, we must also gather the composition and age distribution (and much else) of the group before this is the case and we can make our decisions based on knowledge (*see* Fig. 6.1).

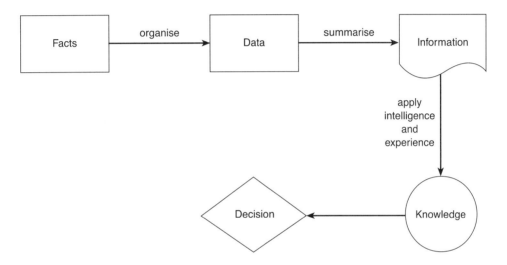

Fig 6.1   Converting facts into knowledge for decision-making

 # Systems

What is a system? The easiest route to an answer is through analogy. We feel comfortable with terms such as digestive system, transport system or computer system. These all suggest relationships and interdependence between parts of a whole. The digestive system is composed of different organs which, although different in form and specific function, all contribute to the digestion of food. Furthermore, the digestive system itself may be considered as just one part (or subsystem) of the larger whole (system) which is the human body.

One of the key features of any system is that the whole is greater than the sum of the parts. Our digestive system is of little use without some means (the skeletal system) of transporting us to where our food lies. Nor is it sustainable without other physiological systems (respiratory, circulatory, nervous, etc.). This completeness or *synergy* is (or should be) the goal of all information system developers. If it is achieved, it tends to be self-reinforcing – each part of the whole 'dancing to the same tune'. For example, if computer technology is matched perfectly to the applications which run upon it, and if its interface to the human beings who operate it is sensitive and intelligently devised, outcomes will generally be positive. If not, vicious circles of decline may set in, where each part of the whole system blames the other as being responsible for any failure.

Components and characteristics of systems

Unless we are dealing with the infinities of the universe, every system is defined by a boundary. Beyond this boundary lies the external environment with which the system connects. This may (literally) be the world outside. More usually, it lies within the organisation of which the system is itself a related and interdependent part. Connection is via an interface. It is this interface which is so often the key to a system's viability. It is the system as others see it. Inputs flow across this interface to be transformed into outputs which flow out into the environment (*see* Fig. 6.2).

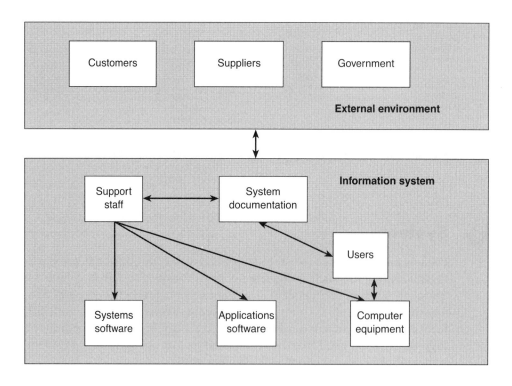

Fig 6.2   An information system and its environment

Management

The advantages of a systems approach lie in the emphasis placed upon inter-dependency between subsystems and in the synergy which is likely to ensue. Managers are the main beneficiaries. They operate at different levels within an organisation.

♦ *Senior management.* This level is concerned with defining organisational strategies and in ensuring the provision of resources with which these may be achieved. It is therefore concerned with the long term. It has the most contact with the external environment.

♦ *Middle management.* The concerns of this level are more with tactical decision-making. The focus is therefore more on the completion of tasks (usually undertaken by staff under their direction) which move the organisation towards the long-term goals set by senior managers.

♦ *Operational management.* This level is most often involved in supervision. Managers at this level try to ensure that the tactical decisions made by middle managers are implemented and also that routine tasks are monitored.

Unfortunately, not every management information system fulfils its primary objective of providing information to these three levels of management. Fewer still go further and become integral to the organisational and management structure as a whole. This will only be achieved where information systems strategy and objectives coincide with those of the organisation – an ideal which we will examine further in Chapter 8.

Data

Most organisational activity produces or can be made to produce data. Sales transactions, for example, generate orders and invoices; production is measured in some form of quantifiable unit to produce some kind of return; market research leads to potential customer profiles; records are maintained on company employees; financial transactions are reflected in bank statements and tax returns; and so on.

Data capture

In the early days of computing, data capture or collection was largely a separate, deliberate activity. Companies might design special input forms which would be completed by hand and passed to keyboard operators, who would then translate them into the punched card format necessary for computer input. This was displaced in the 1970s by operators who keyed directly to magnetic tape systems. Nowadays such input is usually direct to computer disk, but there has also been a move to automatic data capture, so avoiding the time delay and cost of using a keyboard.

What factors influence organisations when they are faced with this data input task? The most important questions are as follows.

Is data static or dynamic?

Static data doesn't change a lot. Names and addresses or departmental structures, for example, will usually be keyed in, with any subsequent alterations made in the same way. Dynamic data (e.g. sales or order transactions) is transient. It can still be keyed in, but if companies can capture the information (at point of sale on a computerised cash till), data capture carries no overhead and is available as usable management information without much delay.

Is data historic or in real time?

Computerised cash tills in supermarkets usually connect to central databases which hold stock as well as sales data. Automatic reordering may therefore be triggered at set stock levels. In practice, although not in any normal sense historic, some time does elapse between data capture and this further processing. However, a transaction at an automatic cash dispenser linked to a bank's mainframe or a travel booking made on a travel agent's on-line terminal constitute input data which acts directly upon stored data within the system. This is *real-time* processing. Once the travel agent has made a booking on a particular flight, it is instantly confirmed and locked out to any other enquiry.

Is data available at source in machine-readable format?

Consider again the supermarket point of sale or check-out. Only a few years ago, if you shopped at busy times it would be quite normal to join a long queue while the check-out operator keyed in the price of each item. Nowadays, with near universal bar-coding of goods and the availability of fast bar-code readers, check-out is quick and accurate, while sales information is much more timely and complete.

Is data text or is it graphics based?

Text can either be keyed in or, in certain applications, may be read automatically by optical or magnetic readers. Images, on the other hand, must be scanned in some way. Usually this is via a *flat-bed scanner*, where the object to be scanned is laid flat and scanned by a moving arm to carry out a point-by-point, digital mapping. This mapping, or image, is then stored in the computer for further processing.

Data description

A major task of all management information systems is to set standards against which all data is captured, stored, moved, manipulated and output. These standards must ensure that the data is held in a form and format which is predictable, secure, efficient and transferable, and which permits a minimum of redundancy or duplication. If this is to be achieved, a description of the data, data source and data flows must be made and maintained. This description is referred to as a *data dictionary*. It may be kept as a manual file (or document) or be stored on a computer. In either case, formats and standards vary and need not especially concern us.

In general, descriptions are usually kept on:

◆ *data elements* – items of data which cannot be usefully disaggregated (e.g. a telephone area code or an invoice number);

◆ *data records* – a record is a set of data items which are related and which most often occur together (e.g. a sales record);

◆ *files or tables* – both are sets of similar data records (e.g. a set of sales transaction records);

◆ *the data store* – a set of related files or tables together with their interrelationships (most often referred to as a database);

◆ *processes* (sometimes referred to as *procedures)* – these are the actions performed on input data to transform it into the desired output (e.g. raising an order);

◆ *data flows* – the movement of data between processes or from and to the external environment (e.g. passing a sales order to dispatch).

In fact, the different data types combine in a hierarchy (*see* Fig. 6.3):

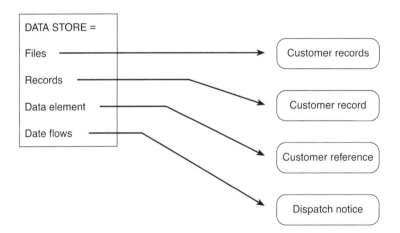

Fig 6.3   Data dictionary hierarchy

data store = set of files

file = set of records

record = set of data elements

element = set of characters (e.g. 0..9, A..Z)

Processes and data flows are these data types in transition (*see* Fig. 6.4).

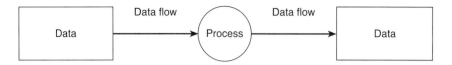

Fig 6.4   Data, data flow and process

Process and data flow

Processes (or procedures) identify and define some activity or task which is carried out on a formal and regular basis and which involves the use of information. Data dictionary entries, describing processes and data flows, are restricted to references to other forms of documentation which define the detail of the procedural logic of a system. This modifies the data and transforms it from input to output.

These definitions of process include:

◆ system structure charts;
◆ program flowcharts;
◆ program code and commentary;
◆ structured English;
◆ decision tables.

The objective in all of these techniques is to specify input and output data flows, together with the logical steps which effect the transformation from one to the other.

At the highest level are structure charts (*see* Fig. 6.5). These present an overview of the system, including all major inputs, processes, storage and output. At a more detailed level (and before programming), system designers need to have specified the process logic, input flows and output flows in precise and unambiguous terms. The specification format or technique used to achieve this varies, and might be one or (more likely) a combination of those listed above.

Let us look at a simple problem and its solution process as it might be specified in structured English, as a program logic flowchart and as a decision table.

In plain English

I want to watch television. So, I must first switch on the television. If the programme showing is acceptable, I sit down, put down the remote control and watch. If there is no acceptable programme, I will read the paper now, otherwise I will read the paper later.

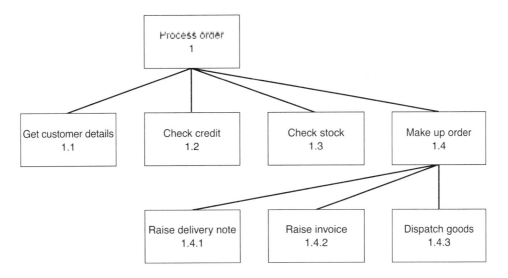

Fig 6.5   System structure chart

In structured English

```
press tv on-switch
repeat
   if program ok    sit down
                    put down remote
                    watch programme
   else             switch channel
   endif
until no more channels or programme ok
press off switch
read paper
```

As a program flowchart

This is shown in Fig. 6.6.

As a decision table

This is shown in Table 6.1.

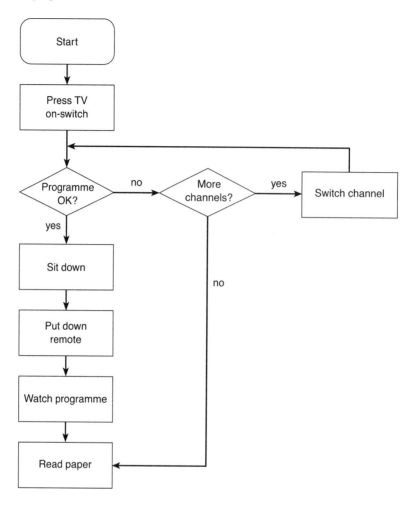

Fig 6.6   Program flowchart

Table 6.1   Decision table

		Rules			
Conditions	Is TV switched on?	Y	Y	N	N
	Is programme OK?	Y	N	Y	N
Actions	Watch TV	X			
	Don't watch TV		X	X	X

Data flow diagrams

These complement the data dictionary and procedural specification by defining the relationships between processes in terms of the data flows which pass between them. If there is one universal technique used by systems analysts, as they progress from descriptions of existing systems to specification of their successors, it is some form of data flow diagram.

Again, we will look at an example. Consider the following process:

◆ Orders from customers come directly or via sales staff.

◆ The orders are validated.

◆ Customer credit details and balances are checked.

◆ Delivery notes are raised (two copies).

◆ One copy of the delivery note is used to raise an invoice which is then sent to the customer.

◆ The customer file is updated.

◆ The other copy is passed to distribution who dispatch the goods to the customer.

This process and related data flows might be represented as the data flow diagram shown in Fig. 6.7.

Conventions vary. In this example, the boxes lie beyond the boundaries of the system as defined by a particular diagram. They are either net originators of data – *sources* – or are net recipients – in which case they are termed *sinks*. Sources and sinks may lie completely outside the system and be located in the external environment, or they may represent subsystems. If they are subsystems, they will be specified in other diagrams.

In all but the smallest systems, the complete set of diagrams will be structured as a hierarchy, with individual sheets showing different levels of detail and cross-referenced to each other. The start point is with an outline (high-level) diagram, but then with progressively increasing detail until further breakdown is no longer useful.

Circles represent processes. Again, these are cross-referenced to more detailed specifications of their logic, written in structured English or defined in flowcharts or decision tables, etc. Arrows denote data flows and can be regarded as pipelines through which packets of data pass, either between processes, or *from* sources, or *to* sinks. Data stores or files are identified with their name within parallel lines.

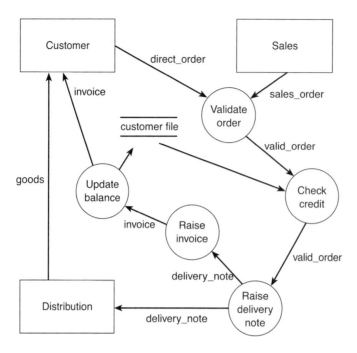

Fig 6.7   Data flow diagram

Systems development

Although all information systems contain data, data flows and processes, only those systems which are developed with *formal* methods are likely to be specified using the techniques described above. This formal approach to information systems development is closely associated with computerisation. It creates the possibility of attaining the design ideal that the computer be made to carry out the work of data capture, organisation, manipulation and output without error or redundancy, and with as little human intervention as possible (perhaps none at all).

What do these formal methods of system specification consist of, and how has the approach to development evolved?

The systems lifecycle model

There have, in fact, been a number of attempts over the years at devising a design method which can create more robust systems and ones more closely geared to user requirements than those associated with the early years of computerisation.

The development lifecycle model emerged in the 1970s. It comprises five distinct stages.

Stage 1 – feasibility study

This is a relatively brief examination of current systems or problems and desired objectives. It looks at alternative solutions within defined parameters. A preferred solution (possibly with alternatives) is put forward, along with a recommendation for the start of a more detailed systems analysis.

Stage 2 – systems analysis

This involves a detailed investigation of the current system. The resulting system description defines all data, data flows, processes, boundaries, specialist staff, operating conventions and documentation. The system's interface with other parts of the organisation and (possibly) external agencies will also be described. During this stage the requirements of a successor system will have begun to emerge.

Stage 3 – systems design

Working on the systems requirements identified at the analysis stage, the systems designer is concerned with detailed specification of all data structures, including the format and content of all input, output, records, files, tables, reports and screen layouts. Procedural logic is also defined. This stage is often iterative (i.e. involves repetition), since user requirements may have been confused or may change as the design proceeds. Final acceptance of the specification allows detailed program definitions to be drawn up and passed to programmers, while any additional or replacement computer hardware acquisition will be put in hand.

Stage 4 – implementation

This stage involves all installation and testing of programs and any new hardware and associated operating systems, documentation and procedure manuals, training needs and any phasing-in requirements. If parallel running alongside an existing system is envisaged, extra resources and staff will be required. If the new system is to go live without any phasing or parallel running, contingencies will need to be drawn up to cater for the possibility and consequences of failure.

Stage 5 – maintenance

This lasts the lifetime of the new system. No matter how exhaustive the testing, programs and documentation will inevitably still contain errors and omissions. In addition, user requirements will change over time, necessitating amendment and revision until (eventually) these are seen to be inadequate as remedies for system failings and the systems lifecycle is repeated.

Weaknesses of the lifecycle model

The main problem with this classic approach to system development lies in the fact that, since the analyst is required to use an existing system as the foundation for any new design, he or she will rarely ask why such a system is required in the first place. Consequently, analysis and design tends to operate only on the surface layers of an organisation. Development takes place along this surface in historical patterns. There may be little or no relevance to current or future requirements and scant examination of the management system for which the information system is designed to serve. Furthermore, if this management system is itself flawed, and is not part of the analyst's terms of reference, any new design is unlikely to succeed and may not even improve on the current one.

Structured methods

These are attempts at overcoming the inherent weakness of the lifecycle model. Structured methods encompass a host of design techniques and development tools, together with an underlying philosophy which controls their use and the nature of the documentation employed. This philosophy also specifies the ways in which projects are managed and staff allocated to different tasks, and (most characteristically) formalises, or *engineers*, the way in which a new system specification is created and documented.

Although they have not yet been identified as such, we have already looked at some of the techniques of structured analysis. Data flow diagrams provide a logical model of different parts of the system. These are accompanied (in the data dictionary) by a definition of organisational data and of the relationships and dependencies within it. In structured design, processes are defined as modules which will then become programs.

Structured programming

This is a method of design which aims to produce efficient and maintainable programs by restricting the programmer's choice of expression. The aim is to replace the 'art' of programming with scientific (or engineering) method, involving adherence to certain language structures and other design constraints. Outcomes are more predictable and errors and omissions less frequent. The approach also facilitates system revision and maintenance, and standardises documentation.

These days, only specialists need to write computer programs, but it is instructive to consider the kind of language which underlies an information system.

The three examples below all define the same simple process (sum, then find the highest of ten numbers input from the keyboard), but by way of comparison are written in BASIC, Pascal and COBOL.

In Pascal

```
program highest(input, output);
{sums, and finds the highest of 10 numbers}

var    num, highest, sum: real;
       n: integer;
begin
  sum : = 0.0
  highest : = 0.0
    for n : = 1 to 10 do
    begin
      read(num);
      if num > highest
         highest : = num
      endif
      sum : = sum + num
    end;
  writeln(' The sum is: ' ,sum);
  writeln(' The highest number is: ' ,highest)
end.
```

In BASIC

```
10      REM SUM & FIND THE HIGHEST OF 10 NUMBERS
20      LET HIGHEST = 0
30      LET SUM = 0
40      FOR I = 1 TO 10
50      INPUT N(I)
60      IF N > HIGHEST THEN HIGHEST = N
70      LET SUM = SUM + N(I)
80      NEXT I
90      PRINT "The sum is: ",N
100     PRINT "The    Highest is: ",HIGHEST
110     END
```

In COBOL

```
IDENTIFICATION DIVISION.
PROGRAM-ID.      HIGHEST.
AUTHOR.          J.SMITH.
DATE-COMPILED.   31/08/96.

ENVIRONMENT DIVISION.
CONFIGURATION SECTION.
     SOURCE-COMPUTER.     VAX 11/70
     OBJECT-COMPUTER.     VAX 11/70
INPUT-OUTPUT SECTION.
FILE-CONTROL.
```

```
                    SELECT INPUT-FILE ASSIGN TO "INFILE"
                    SELECT OUTPUT-FILE ASSIGN TO "OUTFILE"

            DATA DIVISION.
            FILE SECTION.
            FD   INPUT-FILE
                    LABEL RECORDS ARE STANDARD
                    DATA RECORD IS IN-REC
            01    IN-REC                    PIC 9(5)V99.
            FD OUT-FILE
                    LABEL RECORDS ARE STANDARD
                    DATA RECORD IS OUT-REC
            01 OUT-REC                      PIC X(80).
            WORKING STORAGE SECTION.

            ........................
            ........................

            01    HIGHEST-NUMBER      PIC 9(5)V99.
            01    SUM-TOTAL           PIC 9(5)V99.
            01    INPUT-COUNT         PIC 99.

            ........................
            ........................


            PROCEDURE DIVISION.

            100-MAIN.
                    OPEN INPUT IN-FILE
                         OUTPUT OUT-FILE.
                    MOVE SPACES TO OUT-REC.
                    MOVE ZEROS TO HIGHEST-NUMBER.
                    MOVE ZEROS TO SUM-TOTAL.
                    MOVE ZEROS TO INPUT-COUNT.
                    READ IN-FILE
                         AT END MOVE "YES" TO END-OF-FILE.
                    IF END-OF-FILE
                         PERFORM 200-OUT-PUT
                    ELSE
                         IF IN-REC > HIGHEST-NUMBER
                              COMPUTE HIGHEST-NUMBER = IN-REC
                         END-IF
                         COMPUTE SUM-TOTAL = SUM-TOTAL + IN-REC
                    END-IF.

            200-OUT-PUT.
            ........................
            ........................
            ........................
```

As can be seen, there are similarities but also significant differences. Pascal is the most structured of the three. It is taught widely in colleges and universities because of this and the consequent emphasis on good design. However, it is has been less successful commercially. BASIC is simple and is widely used but needed to be significantly enhanced from the original standard for modern development. COBOL is now regarded as a *legacy* system (i.e. it is obsolescent), but many systems written in it are still in place. It is particularly verbose and was originally designed to be as like standard English as possible so that non-experts could use it. (In the example here, quite a few lines specifying how the output is formatted etc. have been omitted. Otherwise the full text would have filled another page.)

Language structures

Sequence (as in a list of statements), *iteration* (as in repetition of a sequence) and *selection* (as in choice of path) are constructs which occur in almost all programming languages. The way they are used, however, may differ, and it is certainly a much more natural process to write structured programs in a language such as Pascal than it is in COBOL or BASIC.

Of the general-purpose languages, C (and its new derivative, Java) is probably the most important, but there are an ever increasing number of database and application development systems available, and also hundreds of specialised computer programming languages, aimed at specific areas of work such as robotics or defence applications, few of which would have much relevance for program development within a management information system.

Prototyping and rapid application development

This is an alternative to the system lifecycle model and, to some extent, cuts across or automates much of the structured methodology. It addresses one of the main criticisms of the lifecycle model, that its approach is inherently linear, i.e. steps must be taken consecutively rather than in parallel. This can lead to delays which often result in systems being delivered based upon the perceived user requirements of two years previously. *Prototyping* and *rapid application development (RAD)* technology aim to eliminate this time delay and at the same time reduce the communication gap between user and developer.

RAD approaches replace some or all of the human input to the design process. They contain routines which automate the production of data dictionaries, data flow diagrams and programs. Program or application generators have steadily replaced much of the chore of the manual coding of programs to a point where it is now possible to create whole systems using visual or graphical design tools. These automatically define the data, process logic, screen layouts and report formats as desired. In addition, many of these environments have integral routines to organise and manage data structures, which, in turn, automate the data dictionary and ensure that data is defined, stored and manipulated in ways which ensure accuracy and security.

In prototyping, early and repeated drafts of incomplete but working systems allow users to gain the 'look and feel' of inputs, screens, reports and outputs. Their feedback influences further development and, with subsequent versions incorporating desired changes and overcoming identified shortcomings, there is a potential elimination of user dissatisfaction and of any failure to meet requirements. Prototyping has only become possible with the introduction of the more powerful programming environments and the development of general-purpose application packages, such as database systems and spreadsheets. In the older programming languages (e.g. COBOL, BASIC, C and Pascal), development is relatively slow, precluding the rapid and repeated drafts the method requires.

The most recent developments centre on the concept of reusable program elements or *objects* and the consequent efficiency gains so realised. These so-called object-oriented languages and associated development systems allow the construction of applications by assembling a set of predefined objects, such as a pop-up dialogue box requesting user input. Since all programs need such an object, once created, it can be used over and over again, saving time and money, and providing guarantees against error since its inputs and outputs are predictable. All mainstream programming languages, together with operating systems such as Microsoft Windows and NT, are now beginning to embrace this new technology. The logical conclusion is to make it possible, eventually, for users to construct their own systems, tailored exactly to need. In this way, word-processor users, for example, may be able to discard large and complex applications such as Word or WordPerfect. Instead, they will be able to assemble their own, customised (and probably far simpler) word processor from predefined objects such as editing routines and spell checkers, etc., which they choose by clicking a mouse pointer on pictures, or *icons*, representing such elements or objects.

Management information systems

We have examined the conceptual background and the development process and are now in a position to look more closely at the finished product. Here, we examine the key features of a successful management information system and also outline some current trends which seem to form the basis for forthcoming technologies.

Management information systems are for managers

It is worth remembering that not all information systems directly provide managers with information and therefore might not be identified as management information systems. Computerised production lines, for example, monitor or control processes, in which outcomes are known in advance and tolerance levels are pre-set. Output from these systems is by exception, i.e. when tolerances are exceeded. However, even here, information accumulated and quantified over a period of time can still be categorised as management information, since it may form the basis at some point for a management decision affecting the production process. Where clerical procedures are automated (e.g. in a computerised stock ordering system), this too can run without human intervention once stock reordering levels are determined. But, again, exceptions would be reported if, say, prices rose beyond set limits, while the summarised information on stock movements over time would also provide input to the decision-making of managers.

Management information systems are formal and computerised

We began by assuming formality and an involvement with computers. In addition, there is the formalised objective of supplying decision-makers with accurate, timely and relevant information. Systems cannot usually make the decisions themselves, but, because information can be accessed at greater speed and in greater volume, the potential exists for more informed decision-making. Note that the additional virtues of appropriateness, accuracy and relevance are not necessarily inherent to a management information system, but must of course be present if the system is to be of any real use.

The key factor for managers is easy, appropriate and accurate information retrieval

Typical users of management information systems are middle rather than senior managers. The responsibilities of middle managers, or supervisors, unlike those of operational staff, generally prevent them from becoming expert users. Consequently, the essence of any system is the interface across which information is retrieved. The more this remains rooted in a reliance on programmers to write queries and reports, the less integrated will a system be with the management process. As we have seen, current developments aim to make such programming redundant by replacing it with an interface to the data which is as close to natural language as is possible.

Unfortunately, this does not yet bring any respite for the world's forests. Even with modern technology and widespread management access to personal computers, much of the information passing from system to managers' desks still takes the form of the printed report. These may be standard reports, i.e. they are produced without request at specified intervals (e.g. stock lists, monthly budget statements, monthly sales figures, etc.). Others may be issued only on demand, and will usually be more specific to a particular problem. For example, a sudden unexplained fall in sales might prompt reporting on sales, broken down by sales representative, geographic area and product type. Exception reports are another type of reporting practice and are issued when some pre-set limit or tolerance is exceeded.

Current trends

Although many reports remain in the traditional computer listing format, they are increasingly being passed to managers via electronic mail, word processors and spreadsheets. This improves presentation and facilitates analysis and statistical modelling. Graphics and segments of other documents can also be integrated.

Users doing it for themselves

Such output will presumably continue to form the basis of organisational reporting. However, for some years now, there has been a trend for the more computer-literate managers to make use of standard database management systems, such as Oracle, Access, Paradox and dBASE. These organise data in such a way that makes it much easier to learn how to extract and relate information, and to generate queries and reports.

User-generated reports and queries may be developed by using:

◆ a proprietary database language (e.g. PAL – for Paradox database systems);

◆ a standard database language (e.g. xbase or SQL);

◆ a graphical querying system (e.g. Microsoft Query);

◆ dynamic links to spreadsheets such as Microsoft Excel or Lotus 1-2-3;

◆ natural language – or close to it.

Mix 'n' match

In these and other ways, management information systems are becoming a diverse mix of :

◆ general-purpose software packages;

◆ dedicated or 'bespoke' applications;

◆ an underlying database management/operating system;

◆ an overlying graphical or natural language interface.

Indeed, there will be a tendency in future for the edges between different elements to disappear as operating systems incorporate more and more features belonging in the past to application packages. The corresponding computer systems on which these will run will be an equally diverse amalgam of networked personal computers, larger central computers and communication links to remote sites and to the Internet (*see* Fig. 6.8). The trick will be to achieve all of this without the user being aware of the underlying complexity.

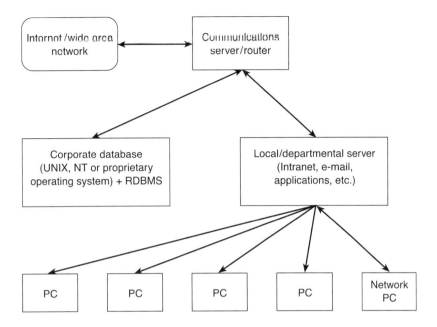

Fig 6.8   Example management information system topology

Power to the user

An associated development has been to give increased power to the user – ultimately to the extent of permitting access to data via the spoken word and video transmission. The use of personal computers, multimedia, the Internet and new operating systems such as Microsoft Windows 95 and NT are all prominent within this context, but there are many other technological advances exerting influence on the ways in which systems work and how efficient managers will find them in use. There have even been a number of attempts at rethinking the concept itself, and of approaching the whole problem of management information from a different perspective. The least radical of these new approaches are *executive information systems (EIS)* and *decision support systems (DSS)*, since both build on earlier designs and possess underlying databases. In contrast, *expert systems* are, together with their research base of *artificial intelligence (A1)*, more radical and revolutionary in design.

Executive information systems

These overlie databases to provide an extra user-layer, which concentrates on providing ease of use to managers who wish to interrogate or construct reports from the underlying data for themselves. In addition to simplicity, other priorities are range and scope. Most users will want to see the wide picture and be able to consult remote, as well as on-site, databases. Information access is always through a graphical interface, and an attempt is made to provide detail at a level appropriate, both to the user and to the problem in hand. A technique known as *drilling-down* is used – to review data at increasing levels of detail until the problem is uncovered or a particular relationship identified. Querying and reporting is automated and graphically based, and is often represented in a spreadsheet-like model – so much so, in fact, that this type of system is often built around a particular spreadsheet such as Microsoft Excel.

Decision support systems

Again, these are closely related to databases and are often linked to executive information systems or spreadsheets, with which they have much in common. Decision support systems go further – in possessing a so-called *model base*. This assists with forecasting, and in the creation and analysis of possible future ('what if') scenarios. Financial modelling and forecasting are the richest fields for this kind of approach. As with related systems, ease of use is paramount, and it is also usual to provide users with a 'global' view of problems. Connection to remote databases, the Internet and on-line news services is consequently often included.

Expert systems

Sometimes referred to as *knowledge-based* systems, these grew out of some aspects of research into artificial intelligence. They depend upon the creation of a special kind of database, or *knowledge base*, which contains, as far as is possible, the acquired knowledge and experience of specialists in a particular field of activity. On top of this knowledge base lies a set of logical ('if-then') rules.

As a simple example, see if you can work out why the following rules would apply to someone who only walked when forced to:

> *if it is warm and dry*
>   *and my car is not available*
>   *and there are not any taxis*
>   *and there are not any buses*
>   *and I can not get a lift from a colleague*
> *then I will walk or not go*

The rule-set is referred to as an *inference engine*. Together with the knowledge base, it allows the interaction between user and computer to follow a more natural path than is normally the case. The interaction takes on the form of a dialogue, in which users are prompted for information and asked questions designed to take them along a logical path to a conclusion.

Although relatively new, especially in respect to management information, the use of expert systems by managers is probably where the future lies, since, instead of merely being assisted in drawing conclusions from processed output, the computer can actually reach its own conclusion and make the decision itself. As computers grow in power and sophistication, and as more confidence is placed in them, a growing amount of decision-making will be carried out in this way. If this is seen as being too mechanical an approach, and as lacking the flair and creativity of the human manager, it is worth saying that it is at least theoretically possible (through a technique known as *heuristics* – 'trial-and-error' or 'rule-of-thumb' approaches to problem-solving) to instil human reasoning characteristics into a machine. Furthermore, computers don't often make mistakes – at least not by themselves.

Although some of the 'hype' surrounding EIS, DSS and expert systems has died down over the past couple of years (to be replaced, unfortunately, by even greater quantities surrounding the development of the Internet and newer concepts such as *data warehousing* and *on-line analytical processing*), the message coming from the following articles shows their growing importance and development.

Undercover Agents

'Everyone agrees that the traditional EIS (executive information system) market has grown far beyond its original definition,' says Ian Meiklejohn, director of conference and report company, Business Intelligence. Today, most organisations are extending both the concept of EIS graphical, screen-based reporting and, in many cases, the actual tools of EIS vendors, to hundreds or even thousands of corporate managers.

An EIS shows key performance data about each section of a company and automatically builds a rolling, up-to-date profile of the business. Its main advantage is that it reduces huge amounts of information down to the essential facts. These days, it also helps any manager look beyond the summaries to obtain the finest level of detail about a particular product, department, or customer.

Thanks to the wide availability of cost-effective access and decision support technologies, most managers have their own database, and need tools to access information held in an assortment of others. They are also big users of e-mail and standard PC software suites. They want an EIS that sits on top of their own system yet works with other management information systems applications to provide business intelligence, be it forecasting, new services, etc. And managers are being forced to collaborate, sharing the responsibility for a project's success or failure.

Much of the technology of the next decade will be oriented to helping people process the enormous quantity of information available to them . . . Expert systems or agent technology . . . are pieces of software that carry out tasks on behalf of the user. [They may] operate at a very basic level. For example, an agent might empty your desktop wastepaper basket at 5 pm each day. However, others are more complex: an agent might assist in a workflow environment annotating documents.

Some agents have the capacity to acquire their knowledge through learning. Data warehousing, a concept which has been around under various names for years, enables companies to store, access and manipulate vast quantities of data, using familiar PC tools. Unlike most corporate database technologies, it specifically supports EIS decision making.

The data warehouse stores all the mission-critical data from a company. With the telecommunications efficiency of the Internet, the ease of use of popular web browsers such as Netscape's Navigator, and the familiar format of a spreadsheet, users can conduct their own *ad hoc* analysis of the latest information.

Source: extracted from *Computer Weekly*, 25 April 1996.

DO-IT-ALL does it all

Do-It-All's senior management team is relying on Planning Sciences' Gentia EIS to help it spot where the company isn't making money. It is currently trying to chop 60 of the most unprofitable stores in the chain and make those it retains more profitable.

Gentia is therefore analysing five main areas of performance . . . 'These decision support applications summarise information in almost any form we want,' says IT and logistics director, Ron Furniss. 'We can even look at the performance of a product group in a re-fitted store and compare it with the same group in a store that hasn't yet had one.'

Source: extracted from *Computer Weekly*, 25 April 1996.

Artificial intelligence

This is the 'Holy Grail'. Research into artificial intelligence began as early as the 1950s, although progress has been relatively slow. Expert systems and robotics are usable off-shoots, but the creation of a 'thinking', 'reasoning' machine still seems a long way off. At present, the major limitation is not so much in software (the language Prolog is particularly promising, for example) but in hardware that is still insufficiently powerful for the demands that would be placed upon it. Nevertheless, the majority of analysts predict that it is just a matter of time before this problem is resolved. Managers will then be 'Spock-like' in being able, with a few simple voice-commands, to have their computers filter mail and calls in order of importance, carry out a full sales analysis, produce and distribute a report, book travel arrangements – and call a robot waiter to bring in the coffee.

Some lines of research into increasing computer power which seem particularly encouraging in this respect are:

◆ *parallel processing* – very fast computer processors linked together allowing simultaneous operation and much higher speeds. These have been used, for example, in trials providing video-on-demand services;

◆ *faster 'chips'* – new materials to replace silicon;

◆ *neural networks* – the claims are that these learn like humans.

Summary

◆ We began with a distinction between *facts, data, information* and *knowledge*, and how a system can be designed to convert facts into knowledge as a basis for reasoned decision-making. In so doing, we examined the concepts of information, system and management as constituent elements of a management information system.

◆ Any system has boundaries which limit its extent and define its interface with the external environment. All but the smallest systems contain smaller subsystems which interact with each other. This interaction takes place in the form of *data flows*. Data enters a system from the external environment or is created from within. It is then transformed by *processes* which modify the data elements as they flow around the system.

◆ Data, data flows and processes are precisely defined within a management information system. This definition or specification takes a variety of forms – among the most common being:

   – data dictionary;

   – data flow charting;

   – process (procedural) flow charting;

   – structured English;

   – decision tables;

   – programming languages.

◆ All the constituent elements of a management information system are put together in a design and development process which usually follows some formal method. The earliest of these (*the systems lifecycle model*) contains inherent weaknesses which have been addressed to some extent by the introduction of *structured methods*. More recently, other alternatives have been developed which allow rapid production of systems through *rapid application development* or via *prototyping*. Both make use of automated environments to reduce the amount of human input and, consequently, the number of errors present.

◆ The completed management information system impacts on operational staff but is primarily designed for different levels of management. Much of the emphasis over recent years is on optimising the quantity, accuracy, relevance and appropriateness of information for each type of user. The development of simpler but more powerful technologies for accessing data is the final prerequisite for the full integration of information system and management. These include executive information systems, decision support systems and expert systems. All of these aim to provide a more natural interface. Artificial intelligence probably constitutes the future of management information system technologies, in which communication between system and user will be via natural language.

Assignments

1 Identify any system with which you are familiar or are a part of. Draw a structure diagram to represent its parts and subsystems and their interrelationships. Define the system's boundary with its external environment.

2 Identify individuals who are representative of the different levels of management. If possible, ask them about their role and responsibilities, and how they see themselves relating to the rest of the organisation to which they belong in the particular context of access to information.

3 Describe in words any clerical, administrative or other logical procedure with which you have some familiarity. Define its internal logic and the data flows which are associated with it. Draw a simple data flow diagram based on your description.

4 Using the logic and data flows identified above, describe the procedure in one of the following ways:

- ◆ program flowchart;
- ◆ structured English;
- ◆ BASIC;
- ◆ any other appropriate language which may be familiar to you.

5 If you have access to computerised data, use whatever retrieval technology is appropriate to generate a query. See if you are then able to integrate the output from your query into a word processor or spreadsheet before printing.

Case study – valuing information

Organisations are increasingly aware of the value of information but find it difficult to quantify this value. In a recent study by Reuters (*see* below), managers were asked to do just this – place a value on their information assets. Most had no idea.

The Reuters study shows that companies are confused about how to go about valuing information as an asset because it is 'intangible and subjective, and its value depends on how it is used'. Form a study/discussion group with colleagues to try to find some answers. Consider the items of information listed here:

◆ a set of final year accounts;

◆ a database of names and addresses structured by age, sex and occupation;

◆ raw quality control data – percentage failure by manufactured part;

◆ raw quality control data – customer satisfaction survey results;

◆ personnel records;

◆ departmental budgets and assets register;

◆ audit results of installed applications on an organisation's PCs.

Although it is not possible to actually quantify the asset in each case, what criteria could we employ to carry us towards such an evaluation?

The output from the group should be in the form of a memorandum to senior management which summarises the difficulties but suggests a way forward based on the outcomes of the exercise.

Getting the best value out of hidden assets

The key to effective information resources management lies in the way in which an organisation looks at its information. Instead of seeing it as an overhead expense, it should be regarded as something of fundamental value, like money, capital goods, labour and raw materials.

Like other quantifiable assets, information has measurable characteristics, namely its method of collection, its uses, and its lifecycle pattern. It is something that can be capitalised or expensed, and controlled by cost accounting techniques.

If information is a resource, it needs to be managed with the same kind of attention that is given to other resources, such as people, money and equipment. This implies that information should not be seen as a free by-product of business operations, but as a significant raw material and product in almost any organisation.

There is another more latent issue that can prevent the development of information resources management policies – information hoarding. In 1994, Reuters commissioned research which demonstrated that most managers in the UK felt they were not always supplied with the information they needed to perform their tasks effectively. They believed that colleagues were withholding information, and that this was impeding their ability to do their job.

Source: extracted from *Computer Weekly*, 9 May 1996, based on 'Information as an asset: the invisible goldmine', Reuters Business Information (1995).

Managing and evaluating information systems

Learning objectives

◆ To discuss the problems surrounding the implementation of change within organisations, and describe some of the approaches which management can take to minimise such problems.

◆ To understand the benefits of using formal project management methods in planning the development and implementation of information systems.

◆ To outline some common techniques used in formal project management.

◆ To differentiate between the roles and responsibilities of different information technology specialists.

◆ To identify ways in which users evaluate computerised systems.

◆ To understand the nature of information systems growth and expenditure over time.

◆ To outline ways in which organisations might quantify the benefits as well as the costs of information systems.

◆ To understand the threats to the security of computerised systems and describe the main preventive measures and ways in which systems might be recovered after disaster.

◆ To be aware of issues of data protection and confidentiality and the main provisions of the Data Protection Act.

So far in this part we have examined the technology which underpins the systematic use of information within organisations (Chapter 5), and have analysed the concept and nature of management information systems (Chapter 6). We can now move on to the management, monitoring and evaluation of these systems, both in their planning and development phase and in subsequent use. In so doing, we will share the same viewpoint as that of all managers whose information needs are to be accommodated. However, the main emphasis is with those who are specifically responsible for assessing the impact of information systems (IS) and information technology (IT), at strategic, tactical and operational levels within the organisation.

Although systems development technologies vary, managers of any project which brings together people and resources in a process of change face similar sets of problems and opportunities. We start therefore with the process of change itself, and look at the problems and approaches of those responsible for its management. It is usually in this early stage that the foundations and framework for future system management, evaluation and control are laid.

Managing change

Any manager responsible for introducing change is likely to be confronted with a wide variety of problems. The area of greatest difficulty is most often associated with the social and psychological effects of change itself – and with the consequent resistance from affected staff.

Resistance to change

People are resistant to change at work for a variety of reasons:

◆ any change can lead to increased pressure on the individual;

◆ existing skills may become outmoded and redundant;

◆ existing authority and status may be put into question;

◆ retraining may be necessary – and this is often a difficult and worrying prospect, especially for older staff.

Such reactions reflect attitudes to change which manifest themselves in everyday life. Some people adapt easily to innovation. They welcome, and thrive upon, changing conditions, situations and the accompanying opportunities. As their experience builds, however, their personal investment in the status quo may make them more cautious and conservative. It is quite often this gradually increasing investment which individuals accumulate throughout their lives that lies behind the opposition to new projects, changing roles and revised work practices.

How do we manage and develop an information systems project which results in change – but with the minimum degree of resistance? Let us identify some of the factors which apply whenever change is planned and how these might be addressed.

The first concern of staff is for their jobs

It follows that, if the proposed change is not expected to lead to any job losses, it is best if this is made clear from the outset (and with conviction), so that the spread and influence of rumour may be minimised. If there are to be redundancies then, again, staff need to be told in good time. Given enough notice, it is much more likely that natural wastage, together with the combined efforts of trade unions, staff associations and other relevant agencies, will ease negative effects and resolve individual difficulties as they arise.

Social and psychological benefits of work

The non-monetary benefits which people gain from work and from working relationships need to be recognised and given due significance in any planned change. Even where individual skills become redundant, it is often possible (through group retraining) to maintain work groups and existing relationships within a new system. If not, anxieties can still be addressed, and new working relationships formed, if training programmes take this into account by including team-building elements within courses.

Ownership of change

People will more readily accept changes if they are encouraged to take 'ownership' of them rather than having them imposed from above. Since, in this context, it is not possible to own unless one has contributed in some way to form and content, staff members and work groups need to be consulted as development takes place. Their ideas and anxieties should be taken up, and incorporated into projects, if beneficial. Even where suggestions from staff are not useful, but can be assessed as neutral to planned outcomes, it might still be beneficial to include them on political grounds. If this process of consultation is then continued during and after implementation, staff will retain a feeling that they possess some control over their work environment. Their feelings of ownership of the change (or at least of some aspects of it) are also likely to endure and remain in place to ease further change down the line. They will also engender loyalty to the organisation.

Change is continual

We should be careful not to view organisational change as something which appears as a comet once in a while, visits us and then goes away. Most change is cyclical – involving swings from periods of relative stability to times when major transformations take place. It consequently involves organisations in continuous development around the kind of problem-solving loop depicted in Fig. 7.1.

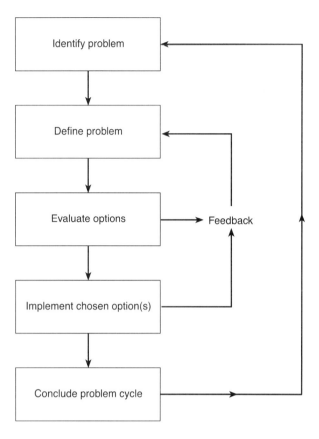

Fig 7.1   Organisational change – a problem-solving approach

At the start of this loop, problems are identified and the need for consequent change recognised. An individual (or group) is given 'ownership' of the problem and charged with the responsibility for its solution. A more detailed definition of the problem and of the change required follows, and then an evaluation of possible solutions. One of these is then implemented – but continuing evaluation continues the cycle as further problems are identified.

Unplanned change

Unfortunately, conditions sometimes exist in organisations which prevent the management of change along any of the systematic lines discussed above. For example, if technological innovation, introduced by competitors, gives them a distinct, competitive edge, markets may be lost irretrievably while the (inevitably) slower pace of negotiated and participative change runs its course. In these circumstances, companies may be forced to opt for a manipulative or coercive approach (often a combination of both), in which staff are kept ignorant of proposed changes but eventually forced to accept them – or suffer consequences of redundancy or loss of earnings and existing conditions.

Managing and controlling projects

Whereas the management of change is correctly concerned with the social psychology of the workplace, project managers are beset with a wide variety of additional problems to overcome and tasks to accomplish – most of them within the further constraint of set time limits. It follows that some attention to planning and control is required for all but the most trivial projects.

Informal approaches to project management

Most people have to manage a project at some point in their lives. It may be a family occasion such as a wedding or a funeral, or some domestic, social, sports or political activity. It might range from home improvement or organising a football competition, to managing a local pressure group or protest action. Rarely are such activities identified in any formal sense as projects. However, more often than not, the individuals responsible for them feel it necessary to think and plan ahead, make lists or schedules, and consider potential obstacles to successful outcomes.

When projects are large or complex a more systematic approach is usually required. Especially where projects are undertaken for business purposes, we would expect to see more formalised techniques. Even here, however, project managers seldom identify themselves as such. Furthermore, although they bring with them to the task relevant skills and experience, most do not possess a formal method or technique which could be applied to the process of project planning and management.

Take, for example, a small building company. From the start to the finish of a project to build a number of houses on a particular plot of land, the builder or site manager will need to arrange for certain conditions, activities and events to be synchronised so as to avoid consequent delay or wastage. Most, if not all, of the activities will be set in a time-frame determined by preceding and subsequent activities. If these take place out of 'sync', problems may arise and extra costs may be incurred.

Most of us are fairly sure that foundations are a prerequisite for walls; walls are prerequisite to the roof. It takes a more professional and experienced eye to recruit (at the appropriate times) the joiners, electricians, bricklayers, plumbers and roofers who are necessary to complete the job to plan. He or she will also need to schedule the purchase and delivery of different materials (again at the appropriate times) to coincide with each stage of development and to avoid wastage or delay. If either condition is not met, and activities occur outside their time-frames, the project as a whole is likely to fail or, at least, be severely disrupted.

Formal project management

Since the majority of information systems development projects are relatively complex, project managers here will be more likely than most to employ some formal planning method to try to ensure:

◆ minimal cost consistent with meeting stated requirements of scope, content, quality and budget;

◆ delivery deadlines are met;

◆ accurate resourcing of people, materials, equipment and finance;

◆ the inclusion of contingencies for unexpected events or delays.

Some of the techniques employed to these ends are discussed below.

Activity schedules

These are, simply, lists of tasks which need to be completed to bring a project to conclusion. The activities are listed in order of completion (although some will run in parallel for some or all of their running time), along with an estimate of time required from start to finish (*see* Table 7.1).

Table 7.1 Activity schedule for an information systems project

Activity	Estimated time (days)
Feasibility study	15
Systems analysis and design	60
Programming	30
Hardware acquisition	15
Implementation and testing	5
Data conversion	2
Staff training	5
System documentation	10

Gantt charts

These plot activities against time and give a graphical comparison of actual as opposed to planned time elapsed, together with an indication of any overlap (*see* Fig. 7.2).

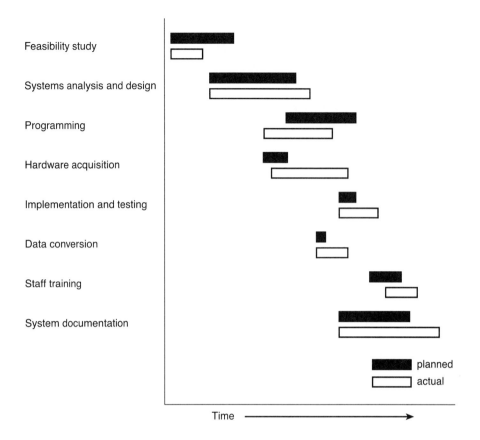

Fig 7.2   Gantt chart

Critical path analysis

If all the activities (and their associated time-frames) critical to the overall success of a project are plotted in sequence against time elapsed, the resulting trace becomes the *critical path* of that project. This critical path (*see* Fig. 7.3) is consequently a measure of the minimum duration of the project. Any change along it will therefore affect the overall conclusion. However, delays in activities not on this path can occur without necessarily causing any overall delay.

Not surprisingly, Gantt charting and critical path analysis are complex procedures for all but the smallest projects. This has encouraged the development of computerised project management systems, some of which are of great power and versatility. Most are designed to help with the management of very large-scale projects, such as civil engineering or defence contracts. On a smaller scale, project management systems which run on PCs are increasingly popular aids to the planning of small to medium scale projects, many of which would not otherwise have received any formal management.

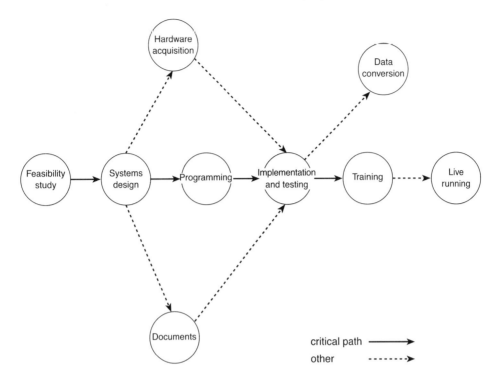

Fig 7.3   Critical path

Managing information systems

Where change and project management strategies properly address issues of resistance and the need for formal planning, they are more likely to incorporate ways in which a new system might be evaluated against cost, monitored for its impact on the organisation and controlled for the maximum benefit of all concerned.

The crucial questions here are:

◆ Who manages the system?

◆ Who evaluates the system?

◆ To whom is the system accountable?

In a perfect world the answer to all three questions would be: *every member of staff in the organisation*. In our imperfect reality, control, evaluation and accountability are either not on general offer or are fought over by groups with quite different perspectives and agendas. In most organisations these may be identified as:

◆ information technology specialists;

◆ users;

◆ managers.

It is possible, of course for individuals to be members of more than one such group, but let us examine their different perspectives.

Information technology specialists

Unless the IT function is provided by an external organisation, in most organisations the same group will be responsible for the development, implementation, management and maintenance of information systems. This is a natural consequence of the specialist skills involved, but it does create its own problems – some of which are unique to information systems. Certainly, many people take the view that those who understand computers do not understand those who do not understand computers.

Although actual job titles and specific roles and responsibilities vary widely, a typical information systems department will possess the kind of structure depicted in Fig. 7.4.

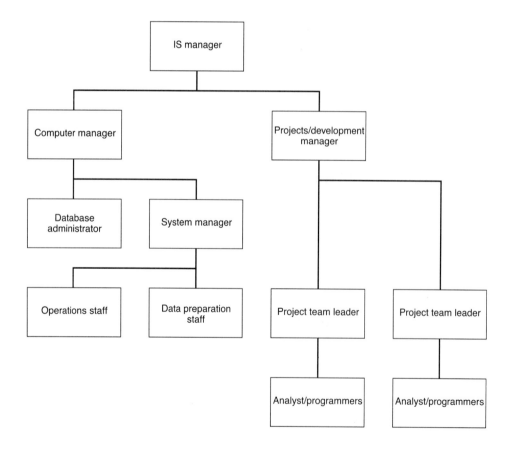

Fig. 7.4   Information systems departmental structure

IS manager

He or she manages the overall operation and development of IS/IT throughout the organisation and, as such, is a service provider to other departments. This position is the pinnacle of career progression for many computer technologists, who, although technically able, may not possess the management and social skills consistent with effective management. Its filling is therefore a crucial factor in the whole process of gaining maximum benefit from the introduction of computerised systems.

Computer manager

This person is responsible for the day-to-day operation and support of installed information systems, but not (usually) for the development of new projects. The job involves supervision over maintenance operations and the provision of technical support for computerised databases, computer hardware and software systems. The computer manager may also be required to manage any data preparation staff.

Database administrator

In some IS departments this is a distinct role and reflects the significance of centralised databases along with the issues of data security, access and integrity outlined in Chapter 5. In others, it may be combined with a network management role.

System manager

Sometimes (confusingly) called a computer manager. In large, multi-user systems and networks, they are responsible for specific operational matters and system access. Since every aspect of operation – from the provision of individual terminals or PCs to user log-in routines, password control, data access and the solution of technical problems – lies within the system manager's area of responsibility, they form the leading edge of the human interface between information systems and their users.

Data managers

They oversee the data-capture operation in larger organisations. The volume of data that has to be keyed in will depend upon the nature of the system and on the stage reached by a particular project. Amounts will be relatively large during implementation, especially where automatic data conversion is not possible and where existing manual records have to be input. When systems mainly involve interactive transactions between operations staff, customers or members of the public (e.g. on-line banking or reservation systems), there is little distinction between this function and normal system operation.

Projects or development manager

This is often a senior systems analyst made responsible for the composition and coordination of different project teams. These teams may be permanent and may concentrate on particular aspects of development, but it is increasingly common for them to be fluid in composition and over time – even disbanding altogether when projects come to an end. Team members will be drawn from analyst and programming staff, but will also include staff coopted from other departments. The latter may bring especially relevant but different skills to a project, or may simply be there to represent the interests of future users. In a more traditional structure, fluid project teams such as these will not exist. Instead, a programming manager, or senior systems analyst, will lead a team of developers employed across a range of different projects. This team would also provide general software maintenance and support for the organisation as a whole.

Whatever the departmental structure, it is always crucial that the functions of control, monitoring and evaluation reside both within and outside information systems departments. Ultimately, the director responsible for IS (frequently the finance director) will have to account to the managing director (and the rest of the board) for overall cost and benefit. However, this is rarely sufficient to ensure that control is maintained at a lower, more detailed level, or that user satisfaction is complete, nor is the appointment of end-user representatives, whose task is to liaise with IT specialists in some kind of user-group forum, where problems of support, training and system performance can be aired and addressed.

The complete answer seems to lie in a full and formal accounting of IS services within service agreements made between IS provider and user departments. In this way, it is possible, to conduct some form of cost-benefit analysis on the provision, and an increasing number of organisations are following this path. Some go one step further by separating the IS facility from the rest of the organisation. It then operates as a separate company within the organisation and 'sells' its product. Alternatively, it may be transferred to a completely separate organisation which specialises in IS provision and consultancy.

This latter process of *outsourcing* – to a facilities management company – is tending to concentrate specialist IT staff in fewer organisations. It can provide the usual benefits associated with economies of scale and simplifies the accounting process, but there is the possible downside of a dependency between an organisation and its service provider.

Users

Whereas the majority of organisations are still far from being in a position to quantify (or even, in some cases, to precisely identify) the benefits obtained from the use of computerised systems, an individual user will usually evaluate on the basis of 'usability'. In fact, to most users, the dialogue (or interaction) between computer and system *is the system*. Consequently, it is this 'front-end' interfacing aspect of a system which, in this context, is most significant in assessing the effectiveness of a particular design.

Usability may be defined more specifically as *human–computer interaction (HCI)*. HCI centres on the nature of the dialogue which takes place between computer system and user. The quality and effectiveness of this dialogue determines to a large extent how much more productive the user becomes, or claims to have become, or has claimed for him by others. Such claims are rarely objective, are mostly intuitive and are too often based on prior expectations or assumptions of benefit. In reality, such assumptions are by no means held universally. There are many critics of the computerisation process as it is carried out in current practice, if not of computerisation itself. There are also many examples of negative productivity effects. Nevertheless, we are probably safe to assume (and most of the evidence is affirmative) that computers help people to work more efficiently, and that, if enough people in an organisation are so positively affected, competitive or other tangible advantage will ensue.

What makes for usability?

We will look only briefly here at some of the ingredients of good interface design which, in turn, contributes to usability. Where these ingredients are omitted, it can cause the average user to position their computer either for best cosmetic effect, or to conceal its real use – as a games machine. They include:

◆ *a natural feel* – the user is not asked to alter his or her approach or order of working. The vocabulary is that of the user rather than one reflecting the operation of the system;

◆ *consistency* – the Windows interfaces for PCs are good examples of consistency within and across applications. Expectations surrounding menus, dialogue boxes, scroll bars and error messages, for example, are always met by these systems;

◆ *no redundancy* – avoiding too many dialogues requesting input that is either unnecessary or might have been obtained automatically from another part of the system;

◆ *on-line support* – help systems which are context-sensitive and which can be retained on screen while tasks are completed. For example, PC users have been 'spoilt' by the inclusion of automated routines such as Microsoft's 'Wizards'. These carry out or guide the user through routine tasks such as mail-merges or setting up a database;

◆ *flexibility* – when a user is new to a system as much help and as many levels of menus, prompts and cues as possible are required. However, as experience and knowledge of the system grows, short cuts are needed. The user learns the key combinations or direct routes to menus which greatly speed up operation and avoid frustration.

Managers

Managers are also users, but they should also be concerned (some especially so) with more general questions of costs and benefit. How may these be quantified, and then placed in relation and comparison with other organisational functions and objectives?

The main requirement is for a measure of benefit to set against cost.

Expenditure

Information technology and information systems do not of themselves generate profit. Instead, they are (like any other organisational function) a charge against profits. IT costs are often particularly high, dwarfing those of other departments. They are also frequently underestimated, and generally increase faster than most other business costs.

Some IT equipment distributors advertise with the slogan: 'Tomorrow's prices today'. This is meant to reflect the continual deflation of equipment prices as technology advances and unit product costs fall. However, this deflation is more than compensated by increasing utilisation, and by exponential rises in the power and functionality of the average system. The latter has broadly maintained its price but with vastly enhanced performance and functionality.

Many organisations have therefore come to resent expenditure on IT. Influenced by a recessionary mood and their own inability to quantify the benefits (and, perhaps, by a number of high-profile project débâcles such as those in recent years at the London Ambulance Service and the Stock Exchange), they have become much more sceptical about the need for any new projects.

Expenditure and growth

Nolan's model of information systems growth and expenditure is still instructive in this context (*see* Fig. 7.5).

◆ *Initiation.* At the outset, spending is flat because the scope for information systems within the organisation is seen to be limited to one or two areas of activity. A good example would be the introduction of word processing. Its initial effects may not be far-reaching and existing work practices are little affected. Expenditure is therefore only modest. However, the benefits of word processors are easily and quickly perceived, and are likely to foster an interest in other benefits which might be realised from introducing computerisation into other aspects of organisational activity.

◆ *Contagion.* Here the benefits of IT are seen (and grasped at) by different parts of the organisation simultaneously. The ensuing pace of development leaves little time to evaluate the benefits of the investment. Amid the general enthusiasm for the technology, expenditure rises dramatically – often exponentially. Poor decisions are made and resources wasted. On the other hand, it is also a time of innovation and great change.

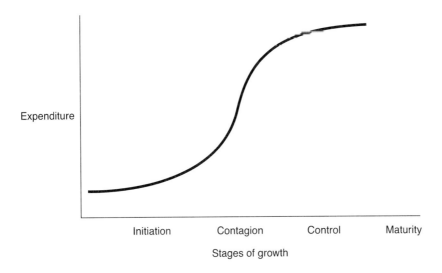

Fig 7.5   Information systems: growth and expenditure over time
(after Nolan (1984))

◆ *Control.* The control stage is reached when those responsible for the allocation of resources realise that IT expenditure has gone out of control. Constraints are now imposed. Proposers of new projects are asked formally (and perhaps for the first time) to estimate costs and to quantify, or at least guarantee, benefits. Budgets are capped, staffing trimmed, and there is frequently a move to formal project management techniques – even some attempt at cost-benefit analysis. Finally, if the earlier stages of growth have been characterised by dispersed initiatives, there is likely to be a reactionary move towards centralisation of the IS function and the imposition of rigid controls. If this has not been the case, and if senior management feels the blame lies with an undisciplined IS department, this may be reduced in size and status, and then placed under the watchful eye of a director, or other senior manager, who is not a specialist in IT.

◆ *Maturity.* In this last stage there is a further reaction – but now to a steadier and more sophisticated approach. The rigid constraints of the control stage are replaced by the setting of realistic objectives and budgets linked to those of the organisation as a whole. Users are given greater influence and control which lead in turn to decentralisation and a more representative set of IT initiatives. Growth still takes place, but within defined strategies and objectives, and within an evaluative and monitoring framework accepted by all concerned.

It is very unlikely that any organisation at any time in its history will fall neatly into this pattern. Indeed, it is likely that some would recognise themselves as proceeding through more than one stage at the same time. It is also worth remembering that companies learn from each other and are influenced by national and international debate. It follows that a company computerising its information systems today need not exhibit the naiveté of those growth stages preceding maturity. It remains, nevertheless, a useful experiential model to employ whenever an organisation begins to review IS requirements – *and* before the genie is let out of the bottle.

Quantifying costs and benefits

The costs of IT are much more easily quantified than are the benefits. The latter are seen (quite incorrectly in most instances) as unquantifiable, due to a lack of criteria against which benefits can be measured. In reviewing approaches to the problem, David Palmer (1994) concludes that benefits arise only when one or more of the following result:

◆ sales volumes increase;

◆ profitability is increased;

◆ costs are reduced;

◆ cost effectiveness is increased;

◆ cash flow is improved.

Palmer (1994) also lists a number of steps which can help in the assessment process:

◆ identify the current value of the outputs from the existing system under investigation;

◆ identify how much that value could be increased;

◆ identify the actions necessary to achieve this increase;

◆ calculate the cost (including the cost of time) of these actions;

◆ compare the relative costs – including those for alternative (perhaps non-computerised) approaches;

◆ implement the most cost-effective actions;

◆ review the impact of these to inform future decisions.

Unfortunately, the first of these alone may require fairly lengthy analysis, and even then provide only an approximation of the costs involved. The other steps may be equally as difficult and imprecise.

Let us look at one of Palmer's examples:

In a new, computerised, sales invoicing system, invoices are raised faster. This leads to improving cash flow and to savings in bank interest. Better information about slow payers leads to reductions in bad debts. Computerised analysis of the customer base and spending patterns leads to improved marketing, reduced stock and less fluctuations in production volumes.

Source: Computer Bulletin, December 1994. Reproduced with permission of the British Computer Society.

All of these can be quantified. If not, asks Palmer, where is the justification in the first place for making the IT investment?

As alternative examples, consider the case for and against the acquisition and use of that most distinctive piece of information technology, the mobile phone. What are the actual needs of two small businesses faced with the task of spending precious start-up funds on essential equipment?

The photographic studio

Its sole owner has premises, already possesses all the necessary photographic equipment, and has also acquired a computer and fax machine. He completes the set-up with the purchase of a mobile phone because he feels in some way that his business will be enhanced if he is always available for contact. In fact, most of his time is taken up in the studio. When he works on location his mobile becomes an inconvenience because it interrupts shooting. So, he switches it off for most of the time. Its main use, he quickly realises, is for social and domestic arrangements and in case of emergency. This may be fine – but it was not his original justification for the acquisition. It is a charge on profits but does little to enhance his business.

The landscape gardener

He calls himself a landscape gardener but most jobs involve standard garden maintenance, lopping trees, and general clearance and tidy-up operations. His working day is very uneven, and he finds himself much of the time driving his van from one job to the next, or back to base for supplies and to check the answering machine. A friend persuades him to invest in a mobile phone, and he quickly realises it brings a bigger and more immediate return on investment than any other item of equipment. He is now able to arrange work on the move. If a job is finished early he can immediately phone the next customer or fit in another. He is more flexible, more efficient and his profits rise. He has no idea how much of this is due to the mobile phone – but he could work it out (with some assistance) if he wanted. The lesson for larger investments and for larger organisations is the same.

The following considerations can also help to quantify costs and benefit:

◆ When costing new developments, the opportunity cost of time spent by the proposed users of the system should be included. If users are provided with more information than is the minimum for their particular requirements, they are prohibited (while absorbing the excess) from engaging in activities more beneficial to the organisation. In particular, it is often said of PCs that their sheer versatility and the variety and ease of information access make them a cause of negative rather than positive productivity change.

◆ When considering alternatives to any new system, the costs associated with these may be discounted against the estimated cost of the proposal. If, for example, to do nothing would result in additional staff costs, then these can be quantified.

◆ Finally, if the benefits of any new system are clear and are quantified, the organisation loses that much money by not developing and adopting it.

We will come to a more strategic view of the benefits of information systems and their integration with organisational structures, missions and objectives in the next chapter. Here we must now turn to a number of other important issues which are associated with using information technology. All relate to questions raised by the heightened profile and significance that data and information assume when computerisation takes place.

 # System and data security

Users of personal computers usually learn the hard way that data, which is not regularly backed up, will one day be irretrievably lost or corrupted. More often than not, this generates no more than a degree of irritability, much retyping and a determination not to let it happen again. In organisational computer systems, the threat and consequences of data loss are more severe. In many cases, systems are 'mission-critical', i.e. are crucial to business survival. Few of us would be surprised if a bank that lost customer records were to get itself into serious difficulties, but many types of business can face ruin if data loss coincides with cash flow vulnerability, or where markets are especially competitive.

What can go wrong?

As you might expect, the list is a long one, for example:

◆ fire, flood, hurricane, earthquake, terrorist attack, war damage;
◆ power failure;
◆ equipment theft and vandalism;
◆ accidental erasure of magnetic storage;
◆ errors in system design and programming;
◆ hacking and other forms of unauthorised access;
◆ virus attack and other forms of deliberate destruction or corruption of software;
◆ fraud.

What is the scale of the problem?

A National Computing Centre (NCC) survey conducted in 1995 gives some indication here (*see* Table 7.2), although it presumably understates the position because of under-reporting.

Table 7.2   IT security breaches (NCC, 1994)

Incident type	No. of incidents
Physical breaches of security:	
1. Computer failure	967
2. Power failure	821
3. Network failure	764
4. Theft	713
5. Lightning	118
6. Flood	46
7. Sabotage	22
8. Fire	15
Logical breaches of security:	
1. Virus	1029
2. Untested or incorrect software	509
3. Computer operator error	424
4. User error	413
5. Misuse of resources/private work	105
6. Other forms of unauthorised access	90
7. Hacking	35
8. Fraud	25

Source: Computer Bulletin, December 1995. Reproduced with permission of the British Computer Society.

The NCC survey also points to hardware and power failures as the most common causes of failure in mainframes and minicomputers, whereas theft and virus attack were most common with PCs. Both theft and virus incidents were increasing, as was fraud. The latter was also the most costly type of incident. Overall, out of an estimated 50 000 significant users of IT, there may have been as many as 30 000 incidents over the two-year period of the survey – leading to a total financial loss of £1.2 billion annually (Middleton, 1995).

Prevention is better than cure

Most organisations accept the need for security measures based on prevention. However, it is generally the larger users that formalise policy and enforce it through agreed and documented practice – and which implement associated sanctions should any breach take place.

The most common preventive measures are discussed below.

Good system design technique

The use of structured methods or other design methodologies (*see* Chapter 6) which reduce the occurrence of logical and other software error should be insisted upon, and adequate documentation should be ensured should a problem still arise.

Passwords

There should be rigorous control of the issue of passwords and regular updates, together with user-profiling to set appropriate access levels and rights.

Job rotation and role separation

This ensures that parts of a system do not become the personal territory of certain individuals – thereby facilitating fraudulent behaviour.

Investigation of all unauthorised attempts at access

This is important whether access has been gained or not. Computer logs will trace all log-in/log-out activity and indicate its location.

Audit trails

These provide auditors with an identifiable trace through accounting and other procedures, which can reveal any deviation in normal patterns of operation signifying possible fraud.

Transaction logging and 'roll-back' operations

These involve the copying (or *dumping*) of data at set intervals. It allows multiple 'undos', and retreat to a specified transaction, or time, if error occurs. This type of procedure includes traditional transaction file generations (*see* Fig. 7.6) in addition to the more sophisticated routines included in database management systems.

Back-up procedures

These involve a back-up schedule which is usually automated on all but the smallest systems. Daily back-ups will only involve active data, but more extensive saves are done at weekly and monthly intervals – culminating in a full system back-up, including all data and the most important system files. All backed-up data is stored in fireproof safes at a separate location away from the computer room or building – sometimes in a bank deposit. In this way, even a catastrophe such as a major fire or terrorist attack will not result in any permanent loss.

Virus protection

This involves a set of rules for handling removable storage media as well as the use of anti-virus software. Computer viruses are programs (or at least segments of program code) which are copied inadvertently into memory from 'infected' discs. Once in memory, they replicate themselves onto any other discs which are accessed, and can also travel across networks. The original infection usually arises from a floppy disc or network file transfer. Effects vary from supposedly humorous but relatively harmless screen displays and messages to the actual destruction and corruption of data and programs.

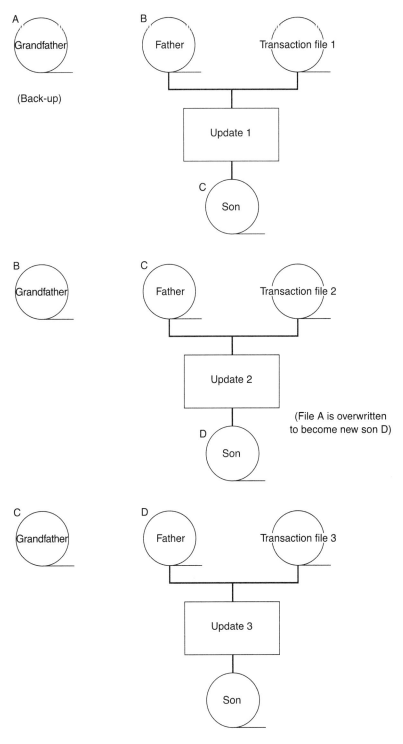

Fig 7.6   File generations

There are more than 10 000 known computer viruses and about 200 new strains are added to this number each month. Most are harmless because they are so poorly written and therefore easily detected. However, there is no doubt a real threat exists. Indeed, in a few cases, real disasters have been caused by virus infections, and in most computer facilities there is at least the overhead cost of protective measures.

The overhead arises mainly from expenditure on virus screening and disinfecting software. These specialised programs are produced by a number of companies who have capitalised on the new and expanding market. There is even a shade of opinion among users that the virus threat has been hyped by some of them so that they can sell more products. Whether or not this is true, such marketing practice could at most be regarded as aggressive rather than criminal. On the other hand, there have also been suggestions that certain virus experts (working for less reputable organisations) are 'gamekeepers turned poachers', and are themselves responsible for particularly damaging and intractable virus mutations.

As the following article shows, the general view of the problem is that, although it has been overplayed, there remains nevertheless a serious threat to IT security. How this is met and dealt with will continue to be an issue of much debate – at least until new operating systems come along which are totally (and intrinsically) immune to virus attack.

Fatal infection?

Twelve years ago an IRA bomb decimated the Grand Hotel in Brighton during the Tory Party conference, imperilling the lives of the then prime minister Margaret Thatcher and her Cabinet. The hotel therefore seems a fitting venue for the Virus Bulletin 96 conference next month as many experts warn that computer viruses can deal a lethal blow to the heart of any computer system.

But is the threat that serious, or are virus-busters talking up the potential danger of infection so that they can offload more of their products on to nervous customers? There are good grounds for users to temper their concern. (Paul) Ducklin (technical manager at anti-virus company Sophos) advises that most viruses pose little threat because they are poorly written.

There's no room for complacency, however. Dr Alan Solomon, founder of anti-virus company S&S International, says: 'If a company has 5,000 net-worked PCs and its staff are sending files to each other constantly, by the time you've cleaned up one end the other side is infected.'

Despite the warning, Solomon believes advances in technology, including the move from DOS to Windows NT and new anti-virus products, may spell the end of the virus threat.

One top security specialist is even more sanguine. 'Viruses are passé,' he scoffs. 'In the great scheme of things they are an irritant more than anything else. At the Brighton conference you will get 150 eggheads in tweeds and thick glasses who are not really in touch with the world. They are Mr Bean types . . . A lot of the trouble about viruses comes from the industry itself where there's a real problem of gamekeepers turned poachers.'

Source: Computing, 15 August 1996.

Virus Top-Ten

	Virus	Type	
1	Concept	Macro	*Macro viruses infect documents. They get*
2	Form.A	Boot	*into the macros (automated routines) of word*
3	Parity_Boot	Boot	*processors and spreadsheets.*
4	AntiEXE	Boot	
5	NYB	Boot	*Boot viruses infect the 'boot sector' of a disk.*
6	Junkie	Boot	*These are the areas of the disk which contain*
7	AntiCmos.A	Boot	*the system data necessary to start or 'boot-*
8	Ripper	Boot	*up' a computer system.*
9	Empire.Monkey.B	Boot	
10	Sampo	Boot	

Source: *Virus Bulletin*, June 1996, extracted from *Computing*, 15 August 1996.

Data encryption

This is the process of codifying data to render it meaningless to unauthorised access. Encryption techniques involve the use of a mathematical process (or *algorithm*) to convert text into a meaningless string of characters. The algorithm acts like a key, which is turned once to codify data, and then turned again to unlock or decode the encryption. Both sender and recipient possess their own private keys. A third (public) key is generated at each encryption process and is held on the network. It is this key which locks out everyone but the designated recipient. A public key might be regarded as a bank's safe-deposit box, in which you have locked away your message. There is only one other key which will open it – that belonging to your recipient. The bank (in this case the public keyholder) should not normally possess a key to the box, but should be able to guarantee its security, even though it resides on a public network.

There is some debate at present about who should be the minder of these public keys. Unless they are absolutely secure, sensitive and financial transactions over public networks (and especially over the Internet) will simply not take place in any significant volume. For example, although virtual shopping malls already exist on the Internet as sites on the World-wide Web (cf. Chapter 6), how many shoppers are prepared to transmit their credit card details over such a public network? More generally, there is the so-called 'non-repudiation' or 'mutual authenticity' problem. How do customers prove they have ordered, and paid for, goods? How do suppliers prove they have fulfilled orders, unless such electronic transactions are so secure that mutual authenticity between sender and recipient is guaranteed, along with total immunity from outside interference? The answers seem to lie in national and international agreement on the holding and holders of public keys. It may be that, in the end, it is only where governments are involved that sufficient trust is generated. This might be at the expense of some fears that tapping powers may then be extended from voice to data networks.

Physical security measures

These include:

◆ back-up power generators;

◆ uninterruptible power supplies which allow controlled shut-down;

◆ controlled access to sites, buildings, rooms and lockable stores;

◆ security video;

◆ alarm systems;

◆ routine shredding of sensitive documents and printer output.

System recovery

Smaller IS facilities can usually protect themselves and recover from any type of systems failure by employing some of these preventive measures, and then relying on system and data back-up tapes to rebuild. In larger installations, and especially where computerised systems are so integral to business activity that any significant *downtime* is unacceptable, organisations need the greater reassurance of a full disaster recovery insurance and strategy. This may involve:

◆ *disc mirroring* – twin disc drives work in parallel, so if one fails the other immediately takes over;

◆ *system mirroring* – a complete duplication of the live system runs in parallel and is available immediately to take over if problems occur;

◆ *standby facilities* – these are arrangements made between organisations running similar equipment, or between user and computer suppliers. They guarantee replacement systems should failure arise. Downtime is limited to the time it takes to restore from back-up tapes;

◆ *insurance* – these pay for replacement equipment and for a team of system rebuilders to work on-site until recovery is complete. An option is to include any trading losses within the cover.

Data protection and confidentiality

During the early 1980s, public fears about the accuracy, confidentiality and 'big brother' aspects of computerised databases encouraged the UK government to pass (in 1984) the Data Protection Act. This brought the UK into line with similar legislation passed in other EC member states. Essentially, it provided for a national register of all holders of computerised, personal data. Registration is compulsory and involves a statement of compliance with the Act's principles of data protection, together with a description of all data held and the reasons for holding it.

The general principles which guide the storage of personal data may be summarised as:

◆ data must not be obtained unlawfully;

◆ data users must declare a purpose for holding personal data;

◆ data which is held must be accurate and not excessive for the declared purpose;

◆ data must be available for inspection on demand by those individuals about whom it is held;

◆ data must be made secure against unauthorised disclosure.

Compliance with the Act also requires that each organisation nominate a responsible member of staff who will monitor data usage and management, and ensure proper access arrangements.

Summary

◆ We began with the problems of implementing change. These arise mainly from staff attitudes. Resistance can be lessened if those responsible for change recognise the significance of:

– concerns over job losses;

– concerns over worsening work conditions and pay rates;

– the social and psychological benefits which people gain from their jobs, and which are often as important as pay;

– the importance of 'ownership' of change.

◆ Most organisations face a cycle of continuous change in which problems are identified and resolved – and then further problems are identified to repeat the cycle.

◆ Information systems projects are often large or complex, and will therefore benefit from formal project management techniques. Some of the more common techniques used are:

– activity scheduling;

– Gantt charts;

– critical path analysis.

◆ Computerised project management systems are available (some for PCs) which make the planning of complex projects much easier than hitherto.

◆ The management, control and evaluation of computerised systems involves users as well as specialist IT staff. Viewpoints differ, with users in particular tending to evaluate systems via criteria of 'usability'.

◆ Managers responsible for expenditure on information systems increasingly recognise the need for control and monitoring. Costs are more easily quantified than are benefits, but it is possible to analyse the latter to gain at least an approximation of benefit to set against cost.

◆ Computerised systems operate frequently at the core of organisational activity. Any failure will consequently result in serious disruption or loss – even to the extent of business closure. It is important to recognise what can go wrong, and to identify measures which will usually prevent a disaster. However, if failure does occur, recovery procedures should be in place to ensure minimum down-time.

◆ Data protection and confidentiality was recognised as a problem in the 1980s. The resultant Data Protection Act of 1984 provides a legal framework for the holding of computerised personal data. Problems of unauthorised access to data have been further highlighted with the growth and development of the Internet. Plans to use this for business and retail transactions are unlikely to reach fruition unless security is assured – probably through the intervention of governments.

Assignment

From either individual or group-based research, write short reports on the problems of organisational change as viewed by:

◆ a managing director;

◆ a manager responsible for IS development;

◆ a manager of an IS user department;

◆ affected operational staff.

Case study

Read the supplementary material below on usability and security.

Take any computer system with which you have some familiarity and:

◆ list the relevant costs;

◆ summarise the benefits;

◆ outline the measures that are employed to prevent data loss and disaster;

◆ outline the steps taken to ensure compliance with the Data Protection Act;

◆ rate the system on criteria of usability.

Surviving a disaster

For a number of years now, SupaSnaps has had a business recovery contract with Hewlett-Packard which provides for a mobile computer room to be made available in the event of a disaster.

[SupaSnaps] have twice had to invoke [this] service. The first time is now a distant memory, but the more recent occasion was in October 1991, still fresh in the minds of those involved.

'Disaster recovery is totally the wrong name,' Paul Hope (Computer Operations Manager) hastens to point out. 'It's really business recovery. If people think it's only for fire and flood they won't think they need it.' In the case of SupaSnaps, the problem was data corruption with no clearly identifiable cause. It would have been foolish to put the users back on without having traced the fault.

Meanwhile there was a business with 357 branches to keep running.

At ten o'clock that Monday night a 42′ articulated lorry pulled into the car park with a full set of brand new replacement equipment. The mobile unit is equipped with air conditioning, an uninterruptible power source, its own generator and a host of features which make it the perfect, self-contained computer room on wheels.

The shutdown occurred on Monday. When the users came in on Tuesday morning they were able to log on to the core system (retailing) as usual. All they saw was the truck outside.

SupaSnaps survived the disaster without losing a minute's trading and with only a very minor interruption to the normal routine of daily business.

Source: Computer Bulletin, June 1995. Reproduced with permission of the British Computer Society.

Little Brother or Big Brother?

Could last week's tragic events in Dunblane have been prevented? In a democratic society, where individual privacy is prized above most other rights, our ability to anticipate and prevent such apparently random acts could be improved – at a price. It's a price greater than many people have thought worth paying: moving society ever closer to the 'Big Brother' state, in which a single image of the nation's citizens, constantly updated from thousands of database sources up and down the country, is made visible to anyone charged with a duty of care towards other citizens – the police, medical centres, local authorities, charities.

That visibility, so vital to those issuing firearms licences for example, could be obtained by linking many of the nation's thousands of disparate, official data sources.

It is one of the ironies of the Dunblane tragedy that Scotland's Central Police is one of the most technologically advanced police forces in the country . . . Central Police does run a 'corporate' database system – known as Total Retrieval Accidents Crime & Events (TRACE) . . . [It includes] a firearms database. But, like those of most police forces, it only holds details on the weapon, who holds it, and where it is housed. That information is not even cross-referenced against the force's criminal intelligence system, let alone any of the thousands of disparate databases up and down the country.

Seen from the perspective of the possible, the issuing of a firearms licence is a completely hit and miss affair.

In today's 'Little Brother' society the checks carried out into individuals applying for gun licences barely scratch the surface.

Technology can carry out far more sophisticated checks than those currently in place. A computer system containing details of every gun-owner in the UK could be linked to a national central register, which is constantly refreshed from many sources.

As soon as a conviction, caution or alert of some kind is registered against an individual holding a firearm, a trigger could alert the issuing force, who could then review and, if necessary, revoke the licence and recover the firearm.

Hamilton undoubtedly had such an extensive history that taking a unified view could have picked up on it. It is probably worth every agency which holds data on UK citizens searching their records so a composite picture of what is known can be constructed to test the 'single image' prevention hypothesis.

Police sources say Hamilton's psychological profile should have sounded the alarm. But, like the Radio 4 listener who revealed that her former husband, a man with psychiatric problems, was given a shotgun licence last year, the fears of everyone concerned can only be allayed if details of all applicants for gun licences are thoroughly database-tested.

That may mean going beyond police systems, which in any case are themselves lamentably fragmented, to medical records, social services and voluntary organisations.

The environment department of local councils might then be expected to put their records of troublesome neighbours into the pot and the name of any individual applying for a firearms licence could be placed in the local newspaper so any local knowledge could be added and researched by the police.

In the aftermath of the Dunblane tragedy, one champion of civil liberties, Harry Cohen, Labour MP for Leyton in London, now agrees there is scope for some form of central register, and that it should be publicly held, rather than be controlled by a privatised agency.

'I'm not convinced checks couldn't be carried out better by the police,' he said. 'But access to their database containing information about suspicions must be very strictly controlled, so that it is only used in the case of sensitive issues, such as gun law and child welfare. Having it in the hands of a privatised agency could be a terrible breach of civil liberties.'

Source: Computing, 21 March 1996.

Today: Little Brother

1. The applicant fills out a four-page application.

2. The authorising officer checks the application against any paper-based records held at the criminal records office (CRO). The name is then entered on a computer and searches are made on the computers of the local CRO and the Police National Computer.

3. Final checks are then made with local collators, normally force intelligence records at divisional level; those records are usually held on a card index and would hold details of any cautions given to an individual.

4. Face-to-face checks are then made on the applicant with local doctors and at the home address to ensure that the gun is not issued to an individual of 'intemperate, or unsound mind, or who is unfit to hold a firearm.'

5. After issuing the licence, these checks are not repeated until five years have passed.

Tomorrow: Big Brother?

1. The applicant fills out a four-page application.

2. Information is then queried from the centre across linked databases using the name, address and date of birth of the individual.

3. Some databases respond with relevant information regarding the individual.

4. Face-to-face checks are then made.

5. Licence holders are continually checked against new national conviction and caution records.

Source: Computing, 21 March 1996.

Should they ever be connected?

Addiction database (e.g. Narcotics Anonymous, AA, Gamblers Anonymous)

Benefit Agency

British Red Cross Society

Department of Social Security (with more than 50 databases)

Driver and Vehicle Licensing Agency

General practitioners (102,000 sets of filing cabinets and local databases)

HM Customs & Excise

Hospitals (1,600 sets of filing cabinets and local databases)

Local authorities (2,000+)

National Fingerprint Identification

National Council for Civil Liberties

National Insurance Records

Paedophile Section of the Specialist Crimes Unit of the National Criminal Intelligence Service

Police forces (43)

Police National Computer

Schools and Universities (20,000+)

Scottish Criminal Records Office

Scout Assoc. Database

Voluntary Organisations and Charities (e.g. Childline, MIND, MENCAP)

Source: Computing, 21 March 1996.

Usability the human factor

Users are getting more uppity by the minute. Nowadays they expect 'in-house' applications to be as 'user friendly' as the output of, say, Microsoft or Lotus.

The Microsofts and Lotuses of this world spend a lot of effort assessing and improving their software in usability laboratories. Until recently, that would have been regarded as a luxury by bespoke developers, but now organisations such as Thames Water are discovering that it is a worthwhile investment.

Jurek Kirakowski is director of Cork HFRG, which has developed Sumi, a method for evaluating 'quality of use' by measuring users' perceptions.

Users try out software in controlled conditions, then answer questions designed to assess software against various definitions of usability.

Responses can be scored by a Windows program, yielding three types of result: an overall usability reading; scores in specific areas (for instance, does the user feel the software is helping them to get the job done?); and comparison with a 'standardisation database' containing scores from existing applications. The responses provide a basis for follow-up discussion with selected users.

Usability comes on stream

Thames Water decided to pilot usability techniques on a large water quality database system, built using rapid application development techniques and client/server architectures. With consultancy input from NPL Usability Services, [the] team worked with developers to make the new system as usable as possible.

'We'd evaluate each prototype heuristically (says Rory Channer, leader of the business systems usability team at Thames), and feed the evaluation into the next stage of the development process.' 'During the design phase, we did paper prototyping, hacking out the screen designs with designers and user representatives. At this stage we were asking questions like: Why do you need all this on one screen? Could the system give you more if we did it this way?'

Another task early in the project was to perform 'context analysis'. Instead of thinking of an ideal user, designers were encouraged to consider the range of different requirements and skill levels that actual users bring to the desktop.

Once there was some reasonably robust software, laboratory techniques were used to quantify usability.

'We've measured the differences in efficiency among different versions of the software. We can say that typical users have saved 20% of their time as a result of this work. Further savings come from fewer helpdesk calls, less systems administrator involvement, and, probably, fewer future releases to correct problems.'

Source: extracted from *Computer Weekly*, 25 April 1996.

Information and the process of management

Learning objectives

◆ To outline different approaches to the study of human decision-making.

◆ To describe the influences on human decision-making of:
   – degrees of certainty;
   – bias;
   – short-term memory.

◆ To describe the influences on organisational decision-making of:
   – 'office politics';
   – 'satisficing'.

◆ To explain the differences between programmable and non-programmable decisions, and identify the structural components of organisational decisions.

◆ To identify general evaluative criteria for assessing the quality of information.

◆ To distinguish the typical information requirements of:
   – top-level (strategic) managers;
   – mid-level (tactical) managers;
   – low-level (operational) managers.

◆ To define and explain a categorisation of information systems strategies which emphasises different interest groups and is encapsulated as:
   – the how;
   – the what;
   – the wherefore and the who.

◆ To define and give some examples of strategic information systems.

◆ To outline factors which tend to discourage companies from implementing strategic information systems.

◆ To understand the importance to organisational success of well-managed and integrated information systems.

◆ To identify developments which might lead in the future to the 'virtual company'.

Having come this far, you should now be able to place a useful perspective (i.e. a positive but sceptical eye) upon information technology and information systems. It has become something of a cliché to speak of information as the 'lifeblood' of organisations, and most of us are well immersed in the idea of the 'information age', even if we are not yet sure about the practicalities involved, or of our part within it.

Organisations need to manage information, and (as we shall see) manage *with* information, if they are to survive and prosper towards and beyond the millennium. The processes of *informed* management have revolutionary potential. Some companies have not yet grasped existing technologies, or have not learned how to manage, control and evaluate them. They will be poorly placed to embrace the new opportunities arising from the maturing of the Internet and the information 'superhighway'.

In this final chapter we will examine the management process itself, and how it is (or should be) embedded in the flow of information. How are decisions made? What determines the relevance and appropriateness of information for different kinds and levels of decision-making? How do organisations develop the ideal of a two-way (duplex) movement of information and decisions from top level to ground – and from ground to top? We will search for our first answers by outlining ways in which human beings make decisions – as far as psychologists and other theorists yet understand it.

Human decision-making

Theories

There are, broadly, two theoretical approaches to the study of how human beings make decisions (*see* Fig. 8.1).

◆ *Descriptive theories*. These try to describe and explain how individuals make actual choices between actual options.

◆ *Prescriptive theories*. These are concerned with optimising decision-making. In what ways can we ensure the most rational options are taken in each particular context, to enable us to move towards our specified objective?

Certainty – uncertainty

The range is from decisions taken under conditions of total certainty (where the outcomes of each choice are known in advance), to decisions for which outcomes are completely unknown.

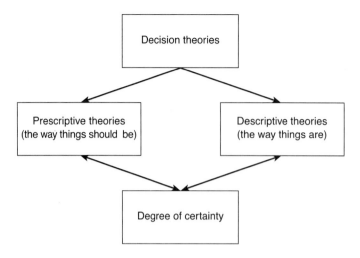

Fig 8.1   Human decision-making theories

In conditions of certainty, the main choices lie between conflicting objectives. For example, if a company reduces staffing levels, costs will be reduced accordingly, but quality of service may also decrease in some quantifiable way. The trade-off is the relative benefit–cost of the decision.

Decisions made with uncertainty cannot be analysed in this way. Since outcomes are unknown it is safest to predict several possible scenarios of cost and benefit. If these are represented as a matrix (with rows showing alternative courses of action, and columns representing possible consequences), we might be able to play out each action a number of times to determine the average return (*see* Table 8.1).

Unfortunately, this model greatly simplifies the process. Even if we were able to plot our options and possible outcomes, and therefore manage in some way to quantify the expected returns so as to select the associated option, we still might prefer to select an irrational alternative – or decline to take any decision at all to avoid risk.

Table 8.1   Payoff matrix

Choices	Expected results (A . . . H) and associated returns								Score
	A	*B*	*C*	*D*	*E*	*F*	*G*	*H*	
Option 1	1	1	0	1	2	2	1	0	8
Option 2	1	1	1	0	0	0	0	0	3
Option 3	0	3	3	3	2	2	0	0	13

Given the 'payoff' predictions outlined in Table 8.1, the rational (if mechanistic) decision-maker would select Option 3 since it offers the best quantified returns.

Bias

Apart of course from his ears, what distinguishes *Star Trek*'s Spock from us mere mortals is his famed logic. His decisions are always based upon informed rationality – if not always made with complete certainty. In reality, we all unconsciously (sometimes consciously) filter information through personal bias and prejudice. In particular, we often prefer and give greater significance to information which is:

◆ *available* – saves the effort of research;

◆ *factual* – concrete evidence, e.g. staff costs, are easily quantified as opposed to intangibles such as public or industrial relations data;

◆ *familiar* – makes us feel more comfortable, e.g. we might give undue weight in making decisions to information based on statistical data if this is structured in ways we have worked with in the past and are therefore most comfortable with;

◆ *recent* – it was said of Mussolini that he always believed the last person he saw – and the latest thing said to him or read by him. Most of us are similarly influenced (if not, fortunately, to the same degree or effect);

◆ *rooted in the past* – almost the opposite effect – the benefits of hindsight. A similar influence is justification after the event. Once an individual makes up his mind he will continue, for some time, to attempt to justify his decision by selecting only information which tends to support it.

Human information processing constraints

Although human beings possess thought processes at which we marvel, and which we find difficult to replicate in computers (e.g. the ability to work with incomplete or imprecise data), we are sadly inferior to the machine when it comes to input and processing volumes, speed and accuracy.

Psychologists generally represent human information processing as the product of three cognitive subsystems: *short-term memory, long-term memory* and *perception* (*see* Fig. 8.2). Our perceptual 'filter' is both physiological and psychological. Whether or not we process information serially (one bit at a time – like a computer), there are definite limits to our input capacity and short-term memory, even if this may not be true of long-term memory.

There is evidence that data is digested in 'chunks'. For example, we remember long character strings such as telephone numbers in segments of three, four or five digits. We also seem able to cope only with a maximum of six or seven items in our short-term memory. Anything larger must be rehearsed and committed to long-term memory if it is to be recalled.

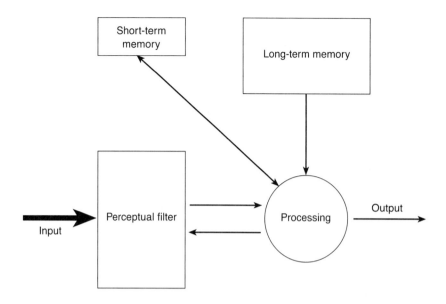

Fig 8.2   Human information processing

 ## Organisational decision-making

General influences

Making decisions within organisations is further complicated by the number of different contributors involved. Most of us accept the existence and influence of 'office politics'. These stem from the presence in most organisations of conflict groups (or individuals), who bring to the decision-making process their own particular bias and agendas. Office politics can sometimes be the most powerful influence, overriding rationality and economic factors. Even where this is not the case, some organisations may (for other reasons) never make a single, perfectly rational and optimal decision in their entire history. Instead, they make suboptimal decisions, designed to 'get by' or 'get them along' – a process known as *satisficing*. They also rarely make decisions which result in a significant change of direction. This tendency to inertia, exhibited in particular by larger organisations, is well documented. IBM, for example, long dominant in the computer industry during the 1960s and 1970s, was presented a challenge in the 1980s from 'upstart' companies such as Microsoft, Apple and Oracle. As a result, IBM suffered a decade of decline before it was forced to restructure and reposition itself in order to survive. (The study material at the end of this chapter looks at this particular case in more detail.)

Types of decision

The simplest and most obvious distinction is between good decisions and bad decisions. Unfortunately, even here, the 'goodness' or 'badness' of most decisions is often (perhaps always) measured subjectively. A more analytical and useful distinction is to see all management decisions as falling somewhere on a continuum ranging from the completely programmable to the completely non-programmable.

Programmable decisions tend to be:

◆ completely informed;
◆ repetitive and routine;
◆ precisely defined;
◆ reliant on rules.

An example of a programmable decision is one concerned with the granting of credit to a customer. Nowadays, most personal loans are made through a process of credit-scoring, involving computer programs which calculate individual scores and make offers accordingly. Human input is merely to add a discretionary element to the process.

Non-programmable decisions tend to be:

◆ incompletely informed;
◆ unclearly defined and unstructured;
◆ novel and sporadic;
◆ made without reference to established rules and practice.

An example of a non-programmable decision might be one concerned (as was the case with IBM) about the restructuring of a company, or with its long-term repositioning within the marketplace.

How many non-programmable decisions might be converted over time into being programmable and therefore made by or with the aid of computer systems? In the answer to this lies the future of information processing.

Components of decisions

Most decisions are probably composed of three distinct subprocesses:

◆ Problems are sought and identified for possible remedial action.
◆ Identified problems are defined and possible solutions generated.
◆ Alternative options are evaluated and a choice made.

The evaluation process in the final stage will be conducted with varying amounts of intuition, subjectivity and objectivity – complete objectivity and rationality being possible only where problems can be defined mathematically. For example, if a company knows (from its own experience) that opening a new local branch office leads to x per cent increase in sales, it can be confident that similar decisions will lead to similar results – subject to any known variations.

Information and decision-making

Now let us consider more closely the information input to the decision-making process. We will look first at general criteria for assessing the value of information, and then go on to consider the different levels of manager, the nature of the typical decisions that they are expected to make and the corresponding information requirements which are appropriate to them. In so doing, we must remember that at the personal level distinctions such as these are arbitrary. In smaller organisations, especially, they are likely to break down as individual managers switch from strategic thinking to tactical or operational matters as the need arises.

Evaluating information – a general perspective

Information cannot exist independently from its recipient. This means that, although we commonly regard an encyclopaedia, for example, as a source of information, it cannot – in the strictest sense – be properly defined as information until someone opens a page and accesses it for a particular purpose. That individual might then use the information so obtained as immediate input to decision-making, or may simply store it in long-term memory for possible future use.

Most learning implies some kind of information storage which at the point of access has potential rather than actual significance. Here, we are more concerned with information which is used more or less immediately to inform decisions. The criteria we employ in assessing its value in this context will vary according to application and with the nature of the decision to be made. In general terms, however, we are likely to evaluate on the basis of the following.

Cost and benefit

Unfortunately, it is often difficult, if not impossible, to quantify the costs and benefits related to a particular item of information, although it can be done in many more cases than are attempted. (*See* Chapter 7 for more on IS costs and benefits.)

Accuracy

Errors which arise in computerised systems may sometimes result in bizarre outputs such as the £1 000 000 gas bill. More common errors are less easy to spot. It has become (sadly) part of the psychology of computer use to implicitly trust information which is printed and well presented as opposed to manual scribbles on pieces of paper. (The obverse, incidentally, lies in the common tendency for customer service staff to blame the computer when anything goes wrong.) In general, we must assume that computer processing, if less sophisticated, is at least more accurate than its human equivalent.

Timeliness

There are few things in life more irritating than being told after an unfortunate event what might have prevented it. Late information in this context is worse than no information at all. If you board a train only to be made aware as it is pulling out of the station that it is taking you to the wrong destination, you must not only suffer the direct consequences of the error, but are also prevented from at least sitting for a couple of hours blissfully unaware of the problem.

Presentation

This may be an obvious point. It is certainly true that most people respond more positively to visually appealing output. In particular, we absorb graphical information more speedily than text. One danger of the computer revolution, though, is the tendency for over-elaboration in output design. How many of us have been forced to wade through acres of gothic font (and the odd cartoon character) to get to information made virtually unreadable by its surrounding (but very artistic) patterned and shaded background.

Conciseness and completeness

We have already seen (Chapter 7) how the explosion of information available on PCs can detract from, rather than enhance, an individual's effectiveness as a manager. In fact, some analysts claim that too much information can make managers ill. Whether or not this is true, if a manager is 'surfing the net' instead of analysing sales figures, then this is clearly an abuse of position and responsibility. A more common problem lies in the distribution of unnecessarily detailed reports and irrelevant subject matter.

Evaluating information – a management perspective

What about the relevance of information? One manager's (relevant) information is probably another manager's (irrelevant) data. Relevance lies in the appropriateness of information (expressed in terms of detail, structure and content) for the particular decision to be made. All managers make decisions, but we have already seen that the nature of these decisions will vary according to the manager's level within the organisational structure. The distinction between strategic, tactical and operational decision-making generally defines these levels, but there are other associated differences. Figure 8.3 illustrates the point.

As we move up through the layers of management function, the effects of decisions made are:

◆ increasingly delayed in their first detectable effects;
◆ felt for longer periods of time;
◆ more significant financially;
◆ made with lower degrees of certainty.

Level of management	Nature of decision	Timescale	Degree of certainty
SENIOR	STRATEGIC	LONG-TERM	LOW
MIDDLE	TACTICAL	MEDIUM-TERM	MEDIUM
SUPERVISOR	DAY-TO-DAY (operational)	SHORT-TERM	HIGH

Fig 8.3   Management levels and decision-making

What are the typical information requirements of managers at these different levels?

Senior managers

Senior managers decide on matters involving strategic, long-term objectives. Consequently, they need outlines, summaries, trends and forecasts. They are often required to relate internal information to conditions operating in the external environment. Therefore, similar outlines, summaries and analyses of industry and economic trends, and of government policy, are relevant.

It is difficult to typify reporting at this level but common examples are:

◆ time-series production and sales charts;

◆ unit costs comparisons;

◆ distribution costs analysis;

◆ profit and loss, cash flow and other financial statements;

◆ labour costs comparisons;

◆ market analyses;

◆ national and international economic trends.

Middle managers

Managers at this level are similarly involved in functions of planning, direction and control. However, their decisions are more short term and tactical. They are aimed more towards the translation of overall organisational objectives (established by senior managers) into the tasks, lists, schedules, budgets and monitoring processes which actually move the organisation along its chosen path.

The associated information requirement is for more detailed reports, often involving comparison of past with present activity. There is also less of a need for external information, since middle managers are less concerned with the outside environment in which the organisation operates than are senior managers.

The particular dilemma in information provision at this level lies in the degree of abstraction. This should be sufficiently high to avoid unnecessary detail – but without seeming to steer the recipient along particular decision paths. In Table 8.2, for example, the spreadsheet analysis of regional sales figures is neutral in that it merely highlights a sharp fall in two of the 12 sales regions (these regions are indicated by an asterisk in Tables 8.2–8.4). The sales manager is alerted to a possible problem.

Table 8.2   Beezer Bits plc: gross sales by region (1996/97)

Region	Total
	(£00s)
One	10 111
Two	12 100
Three	13 270
Four	10 800
Five	14 021
Six	14 300
Seven	6 845 *
Eight	11 050
Nine	10 009
Ten	13 054
Eleven	5 647 *
Twelve	13 023
Grand total	134 230

In Table 8.3, the criteria for analysing staff experience (> 2 years, < 1 year, trainee) should be determined by the middle (sales) manager – not by information systems staff. The addition of salesforce employee data shows that the two problem regions are adequately staffed but have a disproportionate number of trainees and recently appointed staff. The sales manager might consequently decide not to intervene since the information received seems merely to reinforce what would appear to be a natural (and temporary) deviation from the norm. However, the inclusion in a third report – of individual salesperson total sales (Table 8.4) – reveals a different picture. A number of experienced staff in both regions are actually performing poorly, not simply in relation to their counterparts elsewhere, but also in comparison with less experienced staff. The manager, having defined the parameters of the information output, has therefore identified a real problem – and some action is probably warranted.

Table 8.3   Beezer Bits plc: gross sales by region (1996/97) and employee data

Region	Total (£00s)	> 2 years	< 1 year	Trainees
One	10 111	9	1	1
Two	12 100	11	0	1
Three	13 270	10	0	1
Four	10 800	9	3	0
Five	14 021	10	1	1
Six	14 300	11	1	1
Seven	6 845 *	7	3	2
Eight	11 050	11	0	1
Nine	10 009	9	2	0
Ten	13 054	10	0	0
Eleven	5 647 *	6	4	2
Twelve	13 023	9	2	0
Grand total	134 230	112	18	10

Table 8.4   Beezer Bits plc: gross sales by region (1996/97), employee data and individual sales

Region	Total (£00s)	>2 yrs	<1 yr	Trainees	Region Seven staff Sales totals (£000s)	
One	10 111	9	1	1	Bates	298
Two	12 100	11	0	1	Black	840
Three	13 270	10	0	1	Brown (< 1)	670
Four	10 800	9	3	0	Jones (< 1)	556
Five	14 021	10	1	1	Law (Tr)	500
Six	14 300	11	1	1	Mellor	320
Seven	6 845 *	7	3	2	Small	987
Eight	11 050	11	0	1	Smith	239
Nine	10 009	9	2	0	Taylor (Tr)	569
Ten	13 054	10	0	0	Williams	685
Eleven	5 647 *	6	4	2	Winters	329
Twelve	13 023	9	2	0	Wright (< 1)	852
Nat total	134 230	112	18	10	Region total	6 845

Another middle management scenario might be one where a senior management group has decided to standardise all of the company's information systems around, say, Windows NT servers, Intranet and Internet connections and the use of NT or Windows 95 on all PCs. This involves the replacement of obsolete PCs and memory upgrades for most of the rest. The middle manager given responsibility for executing the policy would need to prepare budgets, installation and training plans, and future support and maintenance arrangements. His information requirements consequently include such material as asset register data, sales and technical specifications, staffing and departmental profiles, equipment and software supplier data, and (as in Table 8.5) departmental cost projections for PC memory upgrades and the replacement of obsolete machines. These might be prepared for him by the computer manager, based on the specifications of installed computers and the type of upgrade needed.

Table 8.5   Middle manager's spreadsheet report

Department	386/4	486/4	486/8	586/8	586/16	Upgrade (£)	Replace (£)
One	12	24	32	30	12	8 300	18 000
Two	6	20	31	30	15	7 600	9 000
Three	0	0	40	20	10	5 000	0
Four	20	40	0	0	0	6 000	30 000
Five	10	35	17	0	0	6 950	15 000
Six	0	0	0	30	25	1 500	0
Seven	19	24	0	0	0	3 600	28 500
Eight	0	0	50	10	2	5 500	0
Grand totals						44 450	100 500

Supervisors and operational managers

These managers are responsible for converting the tactical decisions and plans of middle managers into specific day-to-day activities and routines. Using the same example, the requirement in this case would be to translate the decision to upgrade each department's PCs into a schedule of actual upgrades for each machine. The corresponding information requirement would therefore include such documents as inventory listings (*see* Table 8.6), procedure manuals and technical manuals.

Table 8.6   Supervisor's inventory listing

ID	Serial no.	Room/Loc.	Department Two Processor	Memory (MB)	Hard disc	CD
1	5464356	221	486/DX2	4	200	
2	6546654	221	486/DX4	8	500	2X
3	6345634	222	486/DX2	4	200	
4	6456456	222	486/DX4	8	500	2X
5	3456566	222	486/DX4	8	500	2X
6	2435423	222	586/90	8	500	4X
7	2435245	222	586/90	16	500	4X
8	4325246	223	386/DX	4	40	

Organisational strategy and information systems strategy

Remember that (in Chapter 6) we looked at systems in general, and management information systems in particular. We saw that the goal of system planners and developers – even if they sometimes failed to recognise it as such – was *synergy*. Synergy is defined as a sense of completeness, of *integration* – a balance and inter-relationship between subsystems which leads to the whole being greater than the sum of its parts.

One major consequence of integration is loss of identity. We see this in racial matters. There are legitimate fears, on the one hand, that racial integration might result in the loss of cultural specificity, and, on the other, that lack of integration might result in a continuance of discrimination. There is no such dilemma with information systems. Nobody involved with them need ever doubt that a true integration of information systems within an overall organisational system should be the fundamental goal of planners and developers – even where this leads to an identity crisis among computer professionals. It is to an examination of this goal and of ways in which it might be achieved that we now turn.

Organisational strategy

◆ Anything which is strategic touches upon all the activities of an organisation.

◆ Strategy provides a sense of purpose and direction.

This may sound good but we are going to need a little more explanation than this before it is possible to identify some of the factors involved in any attempt to line up information strategy with that of the organisation as a whole. In reality, beyond that of mere survival, organisations pursue many different strategies. They may also define what is strategic in particular ways. The main possibilities can be identified as follows.

Strategy is simply a set of objectives

These are, by nature, relatively stable, i.e. reassessment only takes place in response to major environmental change or fundamental reassessment of resources. Strategic planning involves the defining (and continual refining) of these objectives, together with the major decisions, action programmes and resource allocations needed to reach them.

Strategy is just consistency in our decision-making

This view brings a historical perspective to strategic decision-making. Decisions made over time are a matter of historical record. It is possible therefore to broadly define an organisation's strategy by looking for patterns and similarities (which may indicate coherence and a unity of approach), as opposed to discontinuities. A discontinuous pattern would indicate fundamental reappraisal of objective – perhaps associated with changes in management or ownership.

Strategy is about defining our market

The key aspect of strategic decision-making in this case is to answer the questions:

◆ *What is our market?*

◆ *Is this market changing?*

Market segmentation effectively defines an organisation's territory, within which it competes with others for market share.

Strategy might enable us to gain a competitive edge over rivals

This is concerned with the ultimate company objective of achieving long-term advantage over rivals. It often leads to an analysis of strengths, weaknesses, opportunities and threats (SWOT), carried out internally and on competitors, in a continuous effort to 'stay ahead of the pack'.

Strategy is a means by which we can differentiate managerial roles

This is a way of separating out different strategic perspectives. It puts the different functional responsibilities of senior managers in line with corresponding differences in strategic interest. These different areas of interest can be categorised as:

◆ *corporate* – the highest strategic level which defines an organisation's *mission* (why it exists). Corporate strategy validates all decisions and proposals from other managers, with reference to this mission, and which are strategic in their implications;

◆ *business* – concerned with all major programmes of activity which aim to enhance competitive position;

◆ *functional* – oversees the acquisition and development of all the skills necessary to sustain the organisation. These include:

- finance;

- administration;

- sales and marketing;

- purchasing;

- human resources;

- technology;

- production.

Strategy as a way of defining an organisation's commitment to its stakeholders

The term *stakeholder* has recently moved into the political arena in the UK. It refers to all those who contribute to costs and stand to receive the benefits of organisational activity. These may include:

◆ shareholders;

◆ employees;

◆ customers;

◆ suppliers;

◆ debtors;

◆ creditors;

◆ local and regional communities;

◆ national population and government;

◆ international populations and governments.

The idea is that the organisation defines its strategy on the basis of giving due and appropriate concern to all of these different interest groups.

Information systems strategy

Information systems strategy may also be seen as multi-dimensional. Earl (1989), for example, distinguishes a set of three dimensions. These are encapsulated as the *how*, the *what* and the *wherefore*. The author has added a fourth: the *who*.

Information technology strategies – the how

These are strategies concerned with the technological foundation – for example, computer and network architectures, hardware configurations, operating systems, DBMS, etc.

◆ *How do we set and maintain standards?*

◆ *How do we integrate systems?*

◆ *How do we sensibly upgrade without slavishly following technology?*

Information systems strategies – the what

Here, strategies are aimed at aligning the development of information systems with the needs of business, and, in particular, in using them to gain strategic advantage over competitors. Such strategies are demand-led. They emanate from the user rather than from the technologist.

◆ *What can the system do for the business?*

◆ *What does it do to inform decision-making?*

◆ *What does it do to lower costs?*

◆ *What can it do to increase market share?*

Information management strategies – the wherefore and the who

These are concerned with how information systems are deployed and managed within an organisation. This dimension would also involve the question of what kind of manager or group is given the responsibility for formulating information systems strategy in the first place.

◆ *Who controls IS?*

◆ *Who evaluates new techniques?*

◆ *Who pays?*

This kind of categorisation is a useful analytical tool, but evidence shows that most organisations do not consciously differentiate in this way. We can in fact view most strategies as comprising a mix of all of these dimensions. Furthermore, it is by no means clear if information systems strategies actually are constructed from any objective analysis of the organisation and its environment. Some observers believe instead that strategic plans are assembled (with hindsight) from fragments of corporate strategy, existing assets and previous information technology policies. It may be that IS strategies are built simply by expanding upon past decisions and current assets in line with known organisational goals. In other words, the strategic planning of information system is not a deliberate process.

However, there is still a great deal of evidence which does point to organisations being at least conscious of the need to develop IS strategies in line with organisational strategy. We are therefore going to assume here that rational, objective and integrated IS strategic planning is possible, does exist and will become even more prevalent in the future. Let us go back to Earl's categorisation (and the author's small addition to it) and use it as the basis for identifying some of the problems and possible approaches to the development of IS strategies.

The how

This is the easy part. Strategic decisions which relate to the underlying technology of information systems will often receive emphasis simply because of the number of IT specialists who are normally involved in drawing up strategy. There are, consequently, relatively few organisations which do not possess a thoroughly researched and discussed strategic policy that covers technical and operating standards, supplier and vendor contracting, depreciation and renewal, etc.

The what

Since this involves the rather more difficult and less tangible questions surrounding the integration of information systems strategy and development with organisational objectives, the attention given here is more patchy. The majority of organisations appreciate that a lack of integration often defaults to leaving strategy and development to IT specialists. Some of these may indulge their own preferences, and may move in certain directions because they are either fascinated or familiar with certain (perhaps irrelevant) technologies, or because a particular direction might enhance their individual career prospects. This approach is unlikely to result in integrated systems. On the other hand, many IT managers complain of the short planning timescales (often one year or less) with which they have to contend. How can they make the correct, strategic, medium- to long-term investment decisions given the short-term nature of the business plans within which they must operate?

The wherefore

This is the strategic dimension concerned with the management of information technology and systems. We have already seen that organisations may pursue a centralised or dispersed IS policy – or come to rest at some point along the continuum. Given the trend towards empowering users, the most identifiable movement at present is towards dispersed (or distributed) strategies. In these, user departments are given a great deal of autonomy over resourcing and purchasing decisions – a development coincident with the spread of the personal computer. In most cases of decentralisation there remains a policy of adherence to organisation-wide standards regarding operation systems, applications and database management software, and (perhaps) minimum hardware specifications.

The beginnings of an alternative trend are now discernible in the growth of the Internet and the associated emphasis on networking and shared applications. This may result in a reaction away from decentralisation, or it may (hopefully) lead to a possibly ideal combination of centrally administered and supported distributed systems. Were it to become established, such a strategy would continue the ease of use and innovatory characteristics of personal computing, but with the standards, security, connectivity and information dissemination associated with networks.

The who

Who contributes to information systems strategy, and who is given the responsibility to ensure its integration with corporate objectives? The answer is unclear since there is considerable variability between organisations.

The author well remembers his time working as a computer programmer for a large manufacturing company. All of the firm's information systems had previously been conceived, designed, written and implemented on a mainframe computer by a single individual. This young man had produced no documentation and, since he alone knew the system (from corporate strategy to the last full stop in a COBOL statement), it was not surprising that problems followed his departure. Senior management learned the hard way in this case, and there are still organisations which commit everything to one person. However, for the most part, responsibility for information systems strategy is given to a number of staff – in some cases as many as 10 or 12 (*see* Fig. 8.4). There is also often an insistence that the most senior figure within this group should not be an IT specialist.

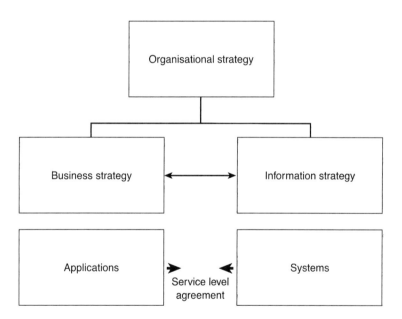

Fig 8.4 Strategic planning teams involved in IS strategy

Strategic information systems

Don't be confused with the overlapping terminology. We have been discussing the desirability and development of IS strategies in line with, and integral to, accompanying organisational strategies. It is only where this process of integration has been pursued to some degree of success that an organisation can ever claim to have created the conditions in which a *strategic information system (SIS)* might be conceived and delivered.

SIS are systems which bring sustained, competitive advantage. Examples include:

◆ electronic share dealing;

◆ computerised news gathering and publishing;

◆ automated banking services;

◆ distribution/transport scheduling systems;

◆ computerised point-of-sale systems.

They are usually innovative, often expensive, high-profile projects. Frequently, they involve:

◆ heavy use of internal resources;

◆ outsourcing and outside consultancy services;

◆ significant restructuring and reorienting of company systems and organisation.

It follows, that as companies adapt to new structures and new ways of operating, SIS can expose them to considerable risk, as well as bring potential benefits.

In addition, to the particular risks involved, there are also more general considerations which might discourage investment in SIS:

◆ Any competitive advantage gained may be temporary. Competitors will quickly imitate, and may, perhaps, be better placed than pioneers since they will have been able to learn from their mistakes. For example, the Tesco supermarket chain, on introducing store loyalty cards, outflanked rival, Sainsbury, but was then, quite quickly, presented with a challenge from a more comprehensive card service. Tesco took up this challenge – and so on.

◆ If the implementation of SIS requires all players in the market to cooperate and coordinate the new systems (e.g. telecommunication standards introduced throughout an industry), little competitive advantage will be forthcoming.

◆ Where consultancy services have been involved, these can also be purchased by competitors – who can then replicate the changes.

IS and organisational success

We have seen (Chapter 7) that, although there are some doubters, the assumption remains that a proper and strategic utilisation of information systems is now crucial to organisational survival and growth. Unfortunately, the case cannot always be made by reference to cost-benefit studies. The most significant benefits of information technology often lie not so much in individual areas such as bad debt or stock reduction or in reduced staff costs (important though such issues are). They seem instead to reside within revolutionised organisational structures and cultures, in which all decisions can be made rationally, and be founded upon information that is relevant, sufficient, timely and appropriate. Some of these decisions (being programmable) will be carried out without human intervention. The rest – more important and those requiring human intervention – will (in such a rational environment) be nevertheless objective and informed.

If much of this still lies in the future for the majority of organisations, there is already a widening gap between those which take the strategic view of IS, and those which do not. Table 8.7 summarises the results of an interesting survey (carried out in 1987 by Brunel University and the Kobler Unit of Imperial College). This highlighted some of the factors which seem to differentiate organisations that possess integrated strategies and those where information systems are marginalised.

The same authors also point to the beginnings of a process in which organisations are built around information systems rather than vice versa. One of their examples is the retailer, Argos. Argos provides a service based upon information. Unlike mail-order firms (which operate in the same market), its systems allow it to carry minimal stock and yet arrange for immediate delivery. The entire operation is made possible and determined by the company's information systems.

An even more radical shift is towards the idea of the 'virtual company'. For some years now, organisations have been flattening management structures and outsourcing more and more of their functions – either to wholly-owned but independent subsidiaries or to completely separate companies. This 'downsizing' strategy has undoubtedly led to leaner and more cost-efficient business units. A similar process has been under way in local and national government. Monolithic, departmentalised structures have been broken down, given autonomy and encouraged to become more competitive. Very few of these changes could have taken place without an accompanying and integral information systems strategy.

The virtual company will take these trends several steps further. The organisation is stripped of all but its core professional and management staff, supported by integrated information systems. Most specialist skills and resources are subcontracted. All other workers are low-skilled, part-time, flexible and distributed. The links are provided by systems which allocate resources, control activities and evaluate performance.

Table 8.7 IS/IT and business success

'Successful' companies	'Less successful' companies

Use of IS/IT – main emphasis

(a) As a business weapon:

'Successful' companies	'Less successful' companies
◆ Response to customers	◆ Improve company image
◆ Improve delivery times	◆ Reduce product price
◆ Improve company image	
◆ After-sales service	
◆ Improve product quality	

(b) As a managerial tool:

'Successful' companies	'Less successful' companies
◆ Faster/better communication	◆ Decision support
◆ Data accuracy	◆ Reduction in staff costs
◆ Faster business planning cycle	◆ Control staff activities
◆ Decision support	

Management of IS/IT

'Successful' companies	'Less successful' companies
◆ Better informed on IS/IT development and use of IS/IT by competitors	◆ Not interested – leave to specialists
◆ Use multiple suppliers	◆ Do not shop around for solutions
◆ Learn from mistakes	◆ Repeat mistakes
◆ Have IS/IT policies linked to business policies	◆ Finance director sets budget – spend is based on user requests, priorities are not clearly defined
◆ Set 'two-year' plans and budgets for IS/IT investment and use steering committees to set priorities based on the strategy	◆ Frame strategies in terms of cost
◆ Frame corporate strategies in terms of customers/products/services	
◆ Top management informed about IS/IT performance – projects appraised before development and after completion	
◆ Separate resources for current operations from future developments	
◆ High spend on education and training of all management and IS staff	

Conclusion

- ◆ There is no correlation between IS/IT spend and business success.
- ◆ There is a good correlation between what IS/IT is used for and how it is managed, and business success.

Summary

◆ We began by looking at the different theoretical approaches to human decision-making. These may be summarised as:

    – *descriptive* – how decisions are actually made;

    – *prescriptive* – how can we best arrive at the most rational decisions.

◆ Decisions are made with varying degrees of certainty of outcome, and it is important to recognise the influences of bias and human information processing constraints upon the decision-making process. In organisations, this is further complicated by non-optimal (satisficing) philosophies and the participation of 'conflict' groups.

◆ Some decisions are programmable, i.e. there is potential for computerisation. Programmable decisions are likely to be:

    – completely informed;

    – repetitive and routine;

    – precisely defined;

    – reliant on rules and established practice.

◆ Non-programmable decisions have few if any of these characteristics and are therefore much more difficult to make.

◆ All types of decision may be structured into three separate stages:

    – identifying the problem;

    – defining the problem along with possible solutions;

    – making a choice between these options.

◆ Information may be evaluated in terms of:

    – cost-benefit;

    – accuracy;

    – timeliness;

    – presentation;

    – conciseness.

◆ The different levels of manager have different information requirements. Senior managers need:

    – outlines;

    – summaries;

    – trends;

    – forecasts;

    – information about the external environment.

◆ Middle managers' reports are, typically, more detailed:

– lists, charts and schedules;

– costings and budgets;

– monitoring and exception reports.

◆ Low-level managers are concerned with day-to-day operations. Typically, they will need:

– job allocations;

– inventories and parts lists;

– specifications;

– procedure manuals;

– technical manuals.

◆ Information systems strategy can be seen as operating within several dimensions. Although the importance of integration is recognised widely, when surface layers are stripped away, relatively few organisations possess a deliberate and systematic process of information systems strategic planning. Instead, planning is loosely based on fragments of organisational strategy and is constrained by current assets and past decisions.

◆ The possible benefits of strategic information systems include the ultimate organisational aim of achieving sustained competitive advantage over rivals. However, the difficulties of pioneering such systems, together with the costs incurred, often discourages companies from attempting to be 'out in front'.

◆ Information systems strategy is now seen to be critical to organisational success. The more this is integrated with that of the organisation as a whole, the more successful a company is likely to be.

◆ The future will probably lie in the further expansion of the role of information systems strategy – eventually, perhaps, towards the information-based 'virtual company'.

Assignments

1 Consider a scale   1 . . . 10 such that:

   1   represents total uncertainty about the outcomes of decisions;

  10   represents complete certainty – all possible outcomes of a decision are known in advance.

Identify a number of decisions you have made and try to score them accordingly.

2 Consider a decision that you (or your group) need to make. Make an attempt at constructing a payoff matrix of all possible outcomes.

3 Read each of the following names with just one pass. Then turn the page and recall as many as you can.

    JENKINSON
    ROWLANDS
    ATKINSON
    MATHERS
    WILSON
    TOMLINSON
    GIBSON
    BANNISTER
    JONES

4 Study the following numbers for no more than two or three minutes. How many of them can you accurately recall?

    34648347837
    78343564758
    13278786776
    23455767676
    78734888435
    92112872439
    31898676107

5 Consider the information requirements of a personnel manager who is given the task of making substantial savings on staff costs over a five-year period. He is aware that adequate funds have been set aside for redundancy settlements, etc. – but must arrive at the end of the set period with annual savings of at least 20 per cent.

What is likely to be the nature and content of the reports that he will require to enable him to carry out the task?

Case study

IBM's recent history shows how a large successful company can lose its way through a faulty strategy, but then rediscover a sense of direction and set new objectives. IBM looked inwards to identify and define the problems, but it also looked outwards for examples of organisations which were operating more successfully – sometimes at the direct expense of IBM itself.

One of these was Microsoft. From the start it possessed a culture quite different from the besuited, corporate image of IBM. The IBM recovery does not of course rest upon the swapping of grey suits for polo shirts. However, the significant differences lay in flat management structures and a devolution of decision-making. Microsoft was more adaptable – less monolithic.

The exercise here is to identify from reading the articles and extracts which follow the most important factors in IBM's revival, and then to turn them, where appropriate, into a set of general recommendations that might apply to other organisations whose relative inertia and conservative management practices have put them at a similar disadvantage. Consider also whether there may be any disadvantages associated with modern management practices and philosophies such as:

◆ flat management structures;
◆ localised decision-making;
◆ outsourcing and facilities management;
◆ less formal communications channels;
◆ fluid management and project teams;
◆ flexible, even casualised labour;
◆ reliance on information technology;
◆ moves towards the virtual company.

Blue-collar worker at the helm

IT WAS just over two years ago that Louis Gerstner resigned as chairman and chief executive of RJR Nabisco, the American tobacco and food giant, to take over the top job at IBM. The computer industry was certainly sceptical about the first chief executive that the deeply inbred IBM had imported from outside the company. Some doubted Mr Gerstner's technical expertise to tackle one of the most daunting problems in American corporate history.

IBM was in a severe mess, with a staggering net loss of $4.9 billion (£3 billion) in 1992. For too long IBM had arrogantly refused to recognise the challenge of smaller and cheaper personal computers to its mainframes. Despite falling profit margins, the company was also too slow to eliminate its lifetime employment practice.

No doubt encouraged by his $5 m (£3.2 m) signing-on bonus, Mr Gerstner quickly set about slashing IBM's high costs and bulging bureaucracy. He also shook up the group's entrenched corporate culture. Its workforce was cut by about 86 000 to 215 000.

From the beginning, Mr Gerstner, 53, made no attempt to hide the fact he was an outsider. On the day of his appointment, he wore an eggshell blue shirt, a subversive fashion statement in the then white-shirted IBM. He would later stun IBM's old guard by doing away with the company's stiff dress code altogether, allowing employees to wear casual clothes.

Early this year, he was able to report IBM earned $2.9 billion for 1994, the first annual profit and revenue growth since 1990. Although Mr Gerstner has engineered a remarkable recovery at IBM, the company is still struggling to tackle the problems in its personal computer business.

Source: The Daily Telegraph, 6 June 1995, © Telegraph Group Limited, London, 1995.

IBM in hostile $3.3 bn bid for Lotus Development

INTERNATIONAL Business Machines, the world's largest computer company, yesterday launched the first hostile take-over bid in its 81-year history when it made a $3.3 billion (£2 billion) offer for American computer software company Lotus Development.

IBM is offering $60-a-share cash for Lotus, causing the struggling software company's shares to soar $28 15/32 to $61 7/32. IBM shares slipped $3 1/4 to close at $91.

If the deal is successful, it will be the biggest software take-over ever and will put IBM in a better position to compete against the industry's leader, Microsoft.

Wall Street speculated that a rival bid could emerge, possibly from Oracle or AT&T, the US telecommunications giant.

IBM last night began legal action against Lotus in an attempt to force the company's board to redeem its poison pill defence mechanism, which makes a hostile take-over prohibitively expensive.

In a letter to Lotus chairman and chief executive Jim Manzi yesterday, IBM chairman Louis Gerstner wrote: "As you know from your conversations with IBM senior vice president John Thompson, IBM has been interested for some time in pursuing a business combination with Lotus.

"Because you have been unwilling to proceed with such a transaction, we are announcing this morning our intention to buy all of Lotus Development's outstanding common shares." Lotus said it will study IBM's offer but said it was "sudden" and "particularly surprising" in the light of negotiations between the two companies during the past several months. The software maker said the talks had included joint development projects.

Lotus has been the subject of take-over speculation for the last six months but this intensified after the company announced a much worse than expected first-quarter loss of $17.5 m.

Analysts had been particularly surprised at a slowing in growth for Notes, Lotus' widely heralded software that lets people work together in electronic groups.

IBM is proposing to finance the offer from its $10 billion (£6.3 billion) of cash. It warned that the acquisition, when completed, will result in a significant one-time charge against IBM's earnings. David Wu, an analyst at S G Warburg in New York, said the deal would dilute IBM's earnings.

"It's a strategic move for IBM. It's dilutive but IBM wants Lotus Notes and it is willing to pay for it," he said.

Patrick Seely, managing director of Broadview Associates, added: "It's another significant step in IBM's development, moving away from hardware. It's a major investment in the software industry."

The deal represents further consolidation in the computer software industry where medium-sized players such as Lotus are finding it more difficult to compete.

Only last week, America's second-largest software company, Computer Associates, announced it was buying software developer Legent for $1.74 billion. Last month Microsoft withdrew its $2 billion offer for Intuit after America's anti-trust authorities said it would block the deal.

Source: The Daily Telegraph, 6 June 1995, © Telegraph Group Limited, London, 1995.

Comment: Windows 95 – When biggest isn't best

The launch of Windows 95 this week is a multi-million pound global event. But as Chris Partridge and Roger Highfield say, this software is a refinement of an imperfect system.

TODAY'S launch of Windows 95 is arguably the biggest event in the history of personal computing. By the end of the year, Windows is expected to have sold 30 million copies – well on the way to matching the 90 million sales of its predecessor, which outsold Michael Jackson's *Thriller*. Yet most people can't explain what it is or does, and those who can regard it as inferior to what has been available for years from rivals such as Apple and Acorn.

To take advantage of Windows 95's strengths, many users will also have to fork out to upgrade existing software and invest in more computing muscle. World-wide, gazillions will be spent adapting to this new standard "operating system", a complex framework that lets you run word processors, spreadsheets, games and other "applications". It makes it easier and quicker to use a personal computer – to add new programs, switch from one program to another or run more than one program at a time.

The promotion costs for the launch of Microsoft's long-awaited operating system could be as much as $400 million, with another $250 million expected to be spent by other companies attempting to ride the wave of Microsoft mania.

In Britain alone, the software giant has spent the best part of £400,000 to buy every copy of *The Times* so it can become Britain's biggest freesheet, adorned with the message "courtesy of Microsoft". For about £8 million, Mick Jagger and Keith Richards have been persuaded to allow their song Start It Up to be used in a commercial that will be shown in 11 countries.

The world's personal computer users now find themselves trapped in a system which is regarded by many as second best.

Tonight, 400 revellers from industry and the media will sit through a Bill Gates video, laser shows and music at a "premiere". On the stroke of midnight last night, bleary-eyed computer bores fought for their copy of Windows 95. Toys 'R' Us and PC World, a subsidiary of Dixons, stayed open until 1am this morning to take advantage of the midnight embargo on sales.

One of the objects of this week's massive global marketing blitz is to lay a smokescreen over the fundamental problem: the world's personal computer users now find themselves trapped in a system which is regarded by many as second best. Indeed the whole business is an instructive lesson in how the free market does not necessarily deliver the best for the consumer. It rejects monopolies, while insisting on uniform technical standards. These conflicting demands can push the consumer to choose technically inferior products. The Windows 95 saga demonstrates that once the consumer has chosen, one system dominates the market. There is no going back. The saga began in the 1970s when the first personal computers were developed by Apple's founders, Steve Jobs and Steve Wozniak. Realising that people wanted to control their own systems and be independent of the vast mainframe computers, they took the newly developed microprocessor chip and incorporated it into a computer system that could be made cheaply and would fit in a box that would sit on your desk. At first the computer industry wrote it off as a toy, but its rapid success forced IBM, the industry leader, to enter the market in 1981.

In those days IBM dominated the industry in the way that Microsoft does now, and it certainly had no inkling that this gadget for hobbyists with ponytails would nearly kill it. For its personal computer, IBM chose to buy, rather than manufacture, the various components including the operating system. Bill Gates was selling one and it was at this point that IBM gave him the world on a plate: the company did not buy him out but simply licensed the system from him, assuming that patents on the hardware would protect them against copying.

Backed by IBM's formidable marketing clout, its PC was a runaway success. Then pirate IBM clones began to appear, at a fraction of official prices. Finally meltdown happened: after many legal actions, IBM lost control of its creation. Companies from Taipei to Telford began making official IBM compatible machines. Prices tumbled. While IBM floundered, Microsoft grew fat on the proceeds of a royalty, vigorously enforced, on every copy of the operating system that every personal computer had to have if it was to be "IBM compatible".

So the prospects are bright for Bill Gates to become one of the richest men in history on the back of a product that no one particularly admires. Apple, meanwhile, had introduced the technically far superior Mac system, based on an easy-to-use pictorial representation. Apple managed to keep control of their own operating system and used that advantage to charge high prices. Buyers chose economy and Microsoft. Today, more than 80 per cent of software written in the world uses Microsoft operating systems.

For all its success, many people (notably non-technical users), were finding the system slow, unreliable and unfriendly. So Gates was faced with the unenviable task of producing an operating system that would catch up with the user-friendliness of Apple while keeping faith with the millions of users of his older operating systems. Windows 95 is the result, and while few would deny that he has achieved both these aims, he has done so at great cost to the consumer.

Whatever Microsoft claims, Windows 95 requires top of the range hardware to fulfil its potential, and this is expensive. Most computer owners will have to upgrade their machines or buy new ones.

Despite this, Windows 95 will be adopted because it caters for the two hot new technologies: multimedia and the Internet. Multimedia has the ability to present information and entertainment on the computer screen in the form of still images, animation, video, sound and text, and computers equipped for multimedia are selling in huge numbers. The Internet is the much hyped world-wide network of information that can be accessed through the telephone line.

Another major attraction to buyers of Windows 95 is that it rectifies a considerable weakness in previous Microsoft systems. Computer games buffs can play their favourite shoot-em-up horrors almost as well as on specialist machines.

So the prospects are bright for Bill Gates to become one of the richest men in history on the back of a product that no one particularly admires; it is little comfort to recall that the free market chose him over his technologically more advanced rivals.

The world is littered with the results of wrong decisions of this sort, of course. If Brunel's broad gauge railway had become standard, the railways might still be able to compete against road transport. The VHS videotape, now ubiquitous, eliminated the superior Betamax format. The pressurised water reactor is the dominant nuclear power source but is neither the safest nor most efficient.

Windows 95 is only the latest in a long, miserable tradition of make-do and mend systems, cobbled up to try to compensate for past mistakes. Like the universal electric plug, the perfect computer is as far away as ever.

Source: The Daily Telegraph, 24 August 1995, © Telegraph Group Limited, London, 1995.

Top executives go in IBM shake-up

LOUIS Gerstner, chairman and chief executive of IBM, yesterday announced a sweeping reorganisation that has led to the unexpected resignations of two key executives.

Robert Labant, a senior vice-president who had run IBM's 35,000 US salesforce, resigned late last week after losing out to Ned Lautenbach in an attempt to run a newly combined world-wide salesforce.

Mr Lautenbach had previously headed IBM's international salesforce.

Mr Labant's resignation comes at the same time as Ellen Hancock, the most senior female executive at IBM, decided to leave after a rival won the top job of overseeing a newly consolidated software division.

In a memo to IBM employees yesterday, Mr Gerstner said that he had created an integrated software group to help the computer giant focus on its software marketing and distribution activities which will be headed by John Thompson.

Mr Labant's and Miss Hancock's departures, which Wall Street analysts believe raises the possibilities of further resignations, also follows the unexpected recent resignation of IBM's treasurer, Frederick Zuckerman.

Analysts believe yesterday's reorganisations may be the most drastic change imposed by Mr Gerstner since he became IBM's chairman and chief executive 18 months ago. He had been criticised for failing to overhaul the company's senior executives.

Source: The Daily Telegraph, 10 June 1995, © Telegraph Group Limited, London, 1995.

IBM golden goodbye offer

IBM, the computer monolith, yesterday announced it was offering voluntary financial incentives for certain US support staff to leave the company.

IBM refused to disclose how many employees had received offers of a payoff, but analysts suggest the move is aimed at getting between 6,000 and 10,000 employees around the world out of IBM's slower growth areas.

Since Lou Gerstner took over as chairman and chief executive to restore the company's fortunes in March 1993, the number of IBM employees worldwide has shrunk by over 76,000 to 225,000, although the company insists a "very small" number of the job cuts were redundancies.

The offer, which is designed to "rebalance the skills" of its workforce, includes two weeks' pay for every year of service at IBM, up to a maximum of 26 weeks and a minimum of eight weeks. The plan also includes a transitional medical programme for up to six months and a reimbursement of up to $2,500 for career transition and retraining programmes.

A spokesman said: "We simply do not know how many will accept." Analysts predicted that IBM may face more lay-offs if not enough staff accept the offers.

However, the company expects its staff level of 110,000 in the US to grow this year as it adds to its computer services business.

Source: The Daily Telegraph, 20 September 1996, © Telegraph Group Limited, London, 1996.

Manzi gives up the ghost at Lotus

JIM Manzi yesterday abruptly resigned as chief executive of Lotus Development, only four months after it was taken over by IBM for $3.5 billion.

In a statement Mr Manzi, 43, who received $77 m cash from IBM for his Lotus shares, said: "I have concluded over the past couple of weeks that I'm not the right person to be leading Lotus at this juncture in its history."

Last June, Wall Street analysts were extremely surprised when IBM said Mr Manzi would remain with Lotus.

Almost everyone had been expecting him to leave as he opposed IBM's hostile bid, only succumbing after the offer was raised. He had also been blamed for much of Lotus' decline.

Some thought Mr Manzi had been persuaded to stay in order to prevent Raymond Ozzie, the star software developer of Lotus Notes, from leaving.

Mr Ozzie had been supportive of Mr Manzi and IBM did not want to upset him. An IBM spokesman said Mr Ozzie continues to work for the company.

Analysts speculated that Mr Manzi had clashed with IBM's top software executive John Thompson. Although Lotus was part of IBM's software division run by Mr Thompson, both men reported directly to IBM's chairman and chief executive Louis Gerstner.

Analysts also noted that Mr Manzi was rather unconventional, in contrast to IBM's stiff corporate culture.

For instance, at Lotus's 10-year anniversary party in 1992, Mr Manzi appeared in drag, mimicking Aretha Franklin and miming to her Motown hit, Respect.

An IBM spokesman declined to comment on the amount of compensation that Mr Manzi will receive. He added that an announcement about his replacement would be made shortly.

Source: The Daily Telegraph, 12 October 1995, © Telegraph Group Limited, London, 1995.

Can IBM shed it stuffed shirt image?

IBM is desperate to change its identity. So it's goodbye to the lumbering, hardware-obsessed corporate behemoth of old, and hello to . . . the new Microsoft?

IBM is attempting to cast off its image as a mainframe supplier, mainly to large corporate users, by taking a leaf out of Microsoft's marketing book.

In preparation for a future that will hinge on distributed computing, Big Blue is focusing on network computing, cross-platform capabilities, openness, ease of use and, above all, the idea that less is more.

'Creating and changing our image is one of our key priorities. Strategy is not the key, implementation is. Microsoft was out fishing with string in the river, while we were fishing with a line in the parking lot. But less is more. In the past, we tried to do everything, when what we needed to do was to walk in rubber boots towards the river,' said Gian Carlo Bisone, IBM's general manager of software marketing.

To set things in motion, Bisone believes IBM needs to . . . focus on ease of use and plug and play.

[Robert Henson, manager of world-wide AIX marketing] talks of addressing usability issues, including IBM's positioning of the Approach database from Lotus as a graphical front end to DB2, which Lotus, in turn, hopes will stimulate sales of its SmartSuite application bundle to IBM users. Notes, meanwhile, will be integrated into all IBM operating systems as the most suitable development environment for the World-Wide-Web.

Bisone summed up IBM's attempted rebirth in typically upbeat fashion.

'There's a new dawn in IT. Network computing is the focus now and the advantage is that everyone's starting from scratch. The leaders last time won't be this time, and network computing plays in the favour of IBM's strongest capabilities. It's back to the future, the sleeping elephant is about to wake.'

Source: Computer Weekly, 2 May 1996. Reproduced with permission.

Glossary

Analogue   Where data is represented by variable physical quantities such as a wave frequency.

Appropriation account   Funds set aside for a specific purpose.

ASCII   A standard codification of alphanumeric characters using binary numbers.

Bandwidth   The difference in a band of radio frequencies. The wider this is the greater the bandwidth and the greater the volume of data that can be transmitted.

Bar code   A representation of data by a sequence of printed bars of varying thickness. Most commonly employed on the packaging of manufactured goods.

Binary arithmetic   Arithmetical operations which use only 0s and 1s to represent any number. Employed in computers because these relate easily to the on–off state of electric current.

Binomial distribution   The frequency of probability that a specific number of successes will result from a number of repeated trials.

Blue-chip   Blue-chip stocks are those belonging to large corporations which have long and consistent records of earnings and dividend payments.

Browser   A computer program which facilitates the location and viewing of hypertext pages on the World-wide Web.

Budget   A financial plan which is used to monitor progress and identify any divergence away from agreed objectives and parameters.

Capital gain   The appreciation in price of an investment.

Capital loss   The depreciation in price of an investment.

Capital structure   The mix of types of finance in a business. The main significance is the proportion of equity to non-equity finance.

CASE   Computer aided systems engineering. Integrated, automated tools for designing and specifying computer software.

Client/server   A type of computer architecture in which the client (desk-top) computer accesses files and applications from a larger, server computer.

Computer virus   A program, or segment of program code, which replicates itself onto discs and within files and documents, causing inconvenience and sometimes data loss.

Corporation   An organisation which is legally separated from members or owners.

Current ratio   This a measure of solvency. It is measured as the current assets of a business divided by its current liabilities.

Data dictionary   A description and specification of all the data residing in an information system. In modern systems this is usually automated and stored on a computer.

Data flow   The movement of data between processes, or to and from an information system and its external environment.

Data flow diagram   A diagrammatic representation of data flows and processes within an information system – frequently used by systems analysts.

Data integrity   The lack of duplication of data in a database. There is only one current and correct version.

Debenture   A bond or certificate acknowledging a debt. They can be bought and sold on the stock market in the same way as shares.

Debt factoring   Transferring all or part of a debt, or responsibility for its collection, to a separate company for a fee or interest.

Digital   Consisting of discrete elements as represented in electronic transmission by on–off states (0s and 1s). These are faster, can be compressed further and are less error-prone than analogue transmissions.

Dividend   The distribution of a company's profits to its shareholders. It is common for businesses to retain part of their earnings for additional investment.

Dividend cover   Earnings per share divided by dividend per share. Any figure above 1 indicates that the business has retained some income.

Dividend yield   Dividend as a percentage of share price. This the actual return for each shareholder.

Earnings per share   The after-tax earnings or profits of a company, divided by the number of the company's outstanding common shares.

Economic order quantity   The order size required to minimise the combined cost of ordering and holding stock.

Encryption   The codifying of data to render it unreadable to unauthorised access.

Equity   Share capital. The risk-bearing finance in a business.

Exchange rate   The rate at which one currency can be traded for another.

Fair market value   The amount a knowledgeable and willing buyer would pay, and a knowledgeable and willing seller would accept – given an open and unrestricted market and no obligation to act. Share prices quoted in daily newspapers, for example, are set at a fair market value.

Fixed cost   A cost which is not proportional to output.

4GL   Fourth generation programming language. More powerful and automated languages, often incorporating database features, and report and screen generators. Common examples are Visual BASIC, Visual C, Delphi, Visual Foxpro and dBASE.

Gearing   The extent to which a business relies on debt finance as opposed to equity finance. A highly geared company is potentially more vulnerable to variations in profitability.

Gross profit rate   The proportion of gross profit to sales. One of the most important measures of a business's basic profitability.

GUI   Graphical user interface. A system such as Microsoft Windows where the user operates a computer via a graphically assisted dialogue.

Intranet   An extension of Internet connectivity and protocols to localised networks – typically an organisation's internal systems. The future seems to lie in systems which allow the use of stand-alone, local network or Internet access without any change to the interface and screens used.

ISDN   A technology for achieving very fast and reliable digital transmissions over existing telephone lines.

Macro   A sequence of instructions which automates a procedure in an application such as a spreadsheet or word processor.

Modem   A device for converting (computer) digital signals to analogue (voice) for transmission along a telephone line.

Normal distribution   The frequency distribution for a variable data-set which can be represented by a bell-shaped curve, symmetrical around the mean value.

OCR   Optical character reader. A device which scans text for automatic input into a computer system.

OMR   Optical mark reader. A device which scans data as marks on a specially printed document.

Open (systems/standards)   In computer systems, used to describe hardware or software specifications which can be supplied by numerous vendors and which can easily integrate with one another. Examples include protocols such as the Internet's TCP/IP, languages such as COBOL or C, and systems which, though originally proprietary, have become open, such as that of the IBM PC standard.

Packet switching   The transmission of data as 'sealed packets' (analogous with letters within envelopes), containing sender and addressee information. These are forwarded by computers *en route* until they reach their destination.

Payback   A way of evaluating a capital project based on the time taken to recover the initial investment.

Portfolio   A collection of investments.

Preference shares   Preferred shareholders receive dividends before ordinary shareholders. If a company closes and goes into liquidation, preference shareholders are entitled to be paid first out of the proceeds.

Principal   The amount of a loan, excluding interest. Loan repayments are usually a combination of principal and interest.

Processor   An integrated circuit which contains and executes all the instructions required for computer operation.

Proprietary   A computer system which originates or is supported by a single supplier. For example, IBM's AS400 or Apple's Mac systems are proprietary.

Protocol   An agreed procedure for regulating the connections between computers.

RDBMS   Relational database management system. A computer system which automatically manages data and facilitates storage and retrieval. Data is held in tabular format of rows and columns.

Relevant cost   A cost which is affected by a decision and is therefore a part of the decision.

Satisficing   A term used to describe the way in which many organisations are content with only satisfactory as opposed to optimal returns.

Sensitivity analysis   A method of measuring which components of a project have the most effect on cash flow if they vary from initial estimates.

Short selling   This means to sell shares and then buy them back later. The shares are effectively borrowed with the anticipation that they will decline in value. If the short-seller is correct, the shares can then be bought back at a lower price to realise a gain. No share certificates are issued nor are lenders named.

SQL   Structured Query Language. A database-oriented language which concentrates on building and maintaining data tables, and which facilitates the generation of queries and reports.

Structured English   A subset of English used to specify a procedure in an information system.

Synergy   Added value realised when component parts (or subsystems) integrate – the whole is greater than the sum of its parts.

TCP/IP   Transmission Control Protocol/Internet Protocol. Communications standards used in Unix networks and the standard protocol of the Internet.

3GL   Third generation programming language. Conventional, high-level languages such as COBOL, BASIC and C.

Unix   The first major operating system to be made available over a range of different types of computer.

Variable cost   A cost which is in proportion to output.

Virtual company   A term used to describe a possible future type of company organisation in which all ancillary services are subcontracted and where most labour is part-time or casual, leaving only the core business managed by a small professional management team.

References and further reading

Beer, M., Eisenstat, R.A. and Spector, B. (1990) 'Why change programs don't produce change', *Harvard Business Review*, November.

Brunel University/Kobler Unit of Imperial College (1987), *The strategic use of IT systems*, London.

Classe, A. (1996) The Human Factor, *Computer Weekly*, 25 April.

Data Protection Registrar (1994) *The Data Protection Act 1984: Guidelines*, Office of the Data Protection Registrar, Wilmslow, Cheshire.

Dodge, R. (1993) *Foundations of Business Accounting*, London: Chapman & Hall.

Earl, M. (1989) *Management Strategies for IT*, Englewood Cliffs, NJ: Prentice Hall.

Gach, G. (1996) *The Pocket Guide to the Internet*, London: Pocket Books.

McKenzie, W. (1994) *Financial Times Guide to Using and Interpreting Company Accounts*, London: Pitman.

Middleton, R. (1995) Computer Security: The Evidence, *Computer Bulletin*, December.

National Computing Centre (1994), *IT Security Breaches Survey*, Manchester.

Nolan, R.L. and Gibson, C.F. (1984) 'Managing the four stages of EDP growth', *Harvard Business Review*, January.

Palmer, D. (1994) 'Justifying IT', *Computer Bulletin*, December.

Parkinson, A. (1994) *Managerial Finance*, Oxford: Heinemann.

Ward, J., Griffiths, P. and Whitmore, P. (1990) *Strategic planning for information systems*, Englewood Cliffs, NJ: Prentice Hall.

Wilson, D.A. (1993) *Managing Information*, Institute of Management Foundation, Oxford: Butterworth-Heinemann.

Index